# Perfect Pets
# ORIGAMI

# Perfect Pets
# ORIGAMI

## John Montroll

Dover Publications, Inc.
Mineola, New York

*To Jan, Igor, and Francis*

*Bibliographical Note*

*Perfect Pets Origami* is a new work, first published
by Dover Publications, Inc., in 2017.


*Library of Congress Cataloging-in-Publication Data*

Names: Montroll, John, author.
Title: Perfect pets origami / John Montroll.
Description: Mineola, New York : Dover Publications, 2017.
Identifiers: LCCN 2016058805 | ISBN 9780486815800 (paperback) | ISBN 0486815803
Subjects: LCSH: Origami. | Pets—Miscellania. | BISAC: CRAFTS & HOBBIES /
  Origami.
Classification: LCC TT872.5 .M675 2017 | DDC 736/.982—dc23
LC record available at https://lccn.loc.gov/2016058805


Manufactured in the United States by LSC Communications
81580301     2017
www.doverpublications.com

# Introduction

**I** love animals, especially, tiny pets. These innocent animals fill our homes with wonder, joy, and companionship. Dedicated to them is this work representing them in origami art.

From aquarium pets, reptiles, amphibians, to birds, mammals, and bugs, there are 33 models. With some practice and dedication, you can have the entire flock in your hands. Best of all, you will not have to feed them or worry if they escape. This variety ranges in difficulty from simple to complex, mostly of intermediate level. Pets include two angelfish, a snake, turtle, parakeet, parrot, guinea pig, pot-bellied pig, hamster, a few dogs & cats, and a complex, but friendly, tarantula. The range of subjects is ideal to add repertoire to a folder's skill. Each model is accompanied by a photo and some information.

Some time ago I pioneered the code where each animal is folded from a single uncut square without any need for glue or tape. As an origami composer, I have tried to make my work fun to fold, with minimal number of steps to capture the details and spirit of each pet. The models can be folded from simple origami paper without being too thick. New folding techniques and structures were developed specifically for these designs. My style captures the animal's proportions with minimal number of layers which gives the models a unique life-force. The elegance and simplicity of this style is highlighted in the guinea pig which takes only 17 steps. Most models can be folded in under 40 steps, keeping it reasonable for the seasoned folder while encouraging the new folder.

In the mammal section are two dogs, a beagle and collie, yet dogs are very popular pets. Where are the dogs? Hold on to your horses, coming soon will be an entire book on dogs in origami, thus complementing this work.

The diagrams are drawn in the internationally approved Randlett-Yoshizawa style, which is easy to follow once you learn the basic folds. You can use any kind of square paper for these models, but I recommend standard origami paper, which is colored on one side and white on the other (in the diagrams in this book, the shading represents the colored side). Large sheets are easier to use than small ones.

Origami supplies can be found in arts and craft shops, or at Dover Publications online: www.doverpublications.com. You can also visit OrigamiUSA at www.origamiusa.org for origami supplies and other related information including an extensive list of local, national, and international origami groups.

I thank my editors, Charley Montroll and Himanshu Agrawal, whose input added much life to this work. I thank Nishant Carr for photographing several models.

John Montroll
www.johnmontroll.com

# Contents

★ Simple
★★ Intermediate
★★★ Complex

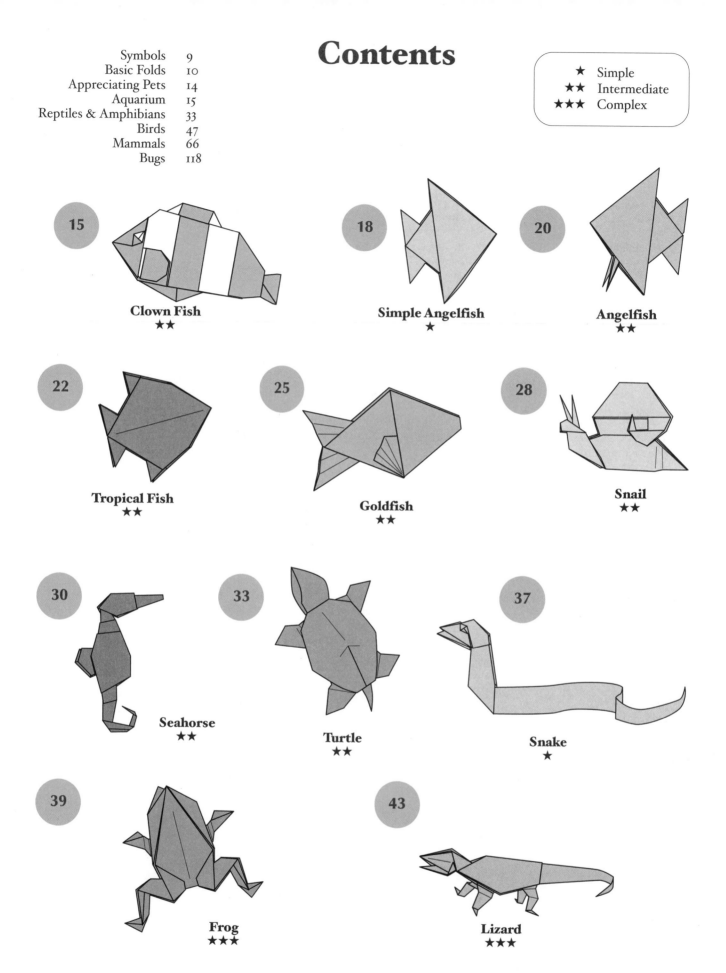

**15** Clown Fish
★★

**18** Simple Angelfish
★

**20** Angelfish
★★

**22** Tropical Fish
★★

**25** Goldfish
★★

**28** Snail
★★

**30** Seahorse
★★

**33** Turtle
★★

**37** Snake
★

**39** Frog
★★★

**43** Lizard
★★★

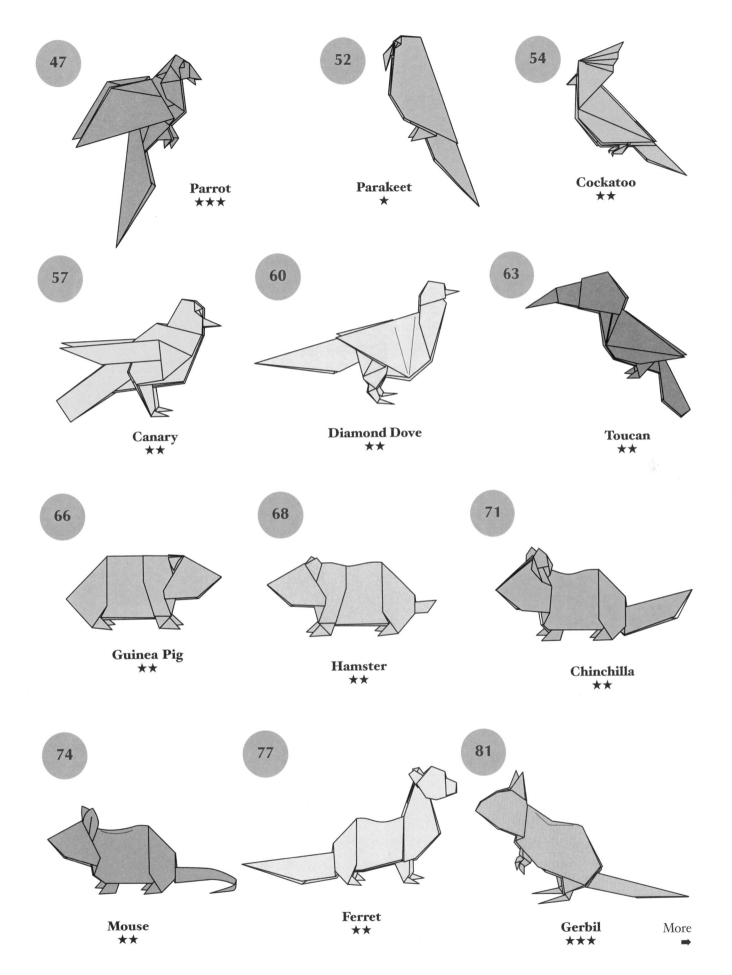

More ➡

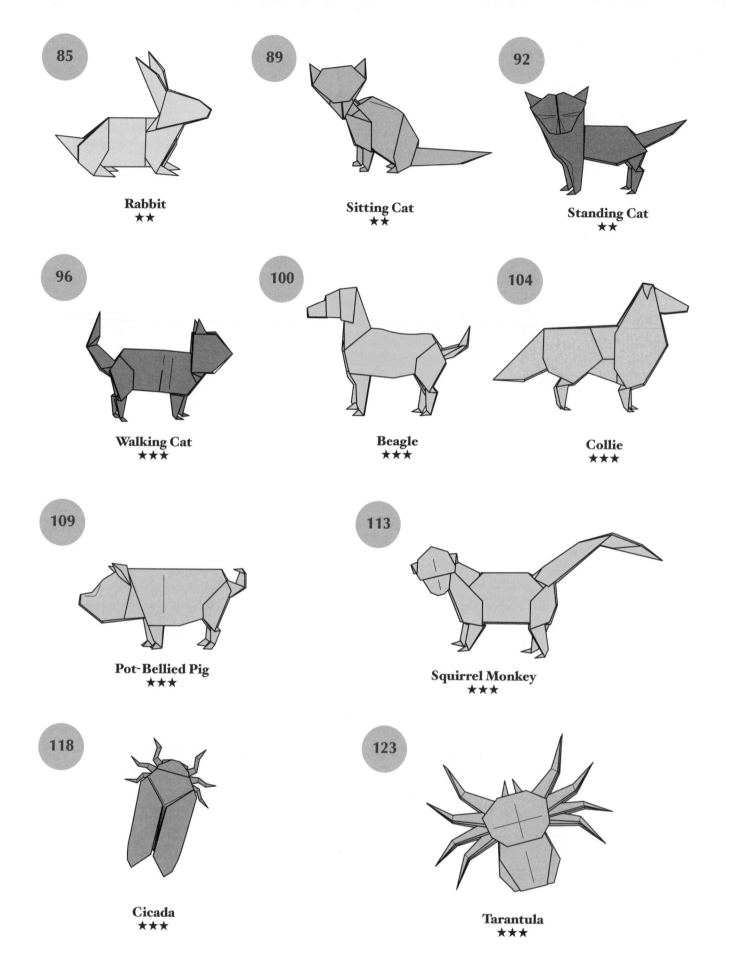

**85** Rabbit
★★

**89** Sitting Cat
★★

**92** Standing Cat
★★

**96** Walking Cat
★★★

**100** Beagle
★★★

**104** Collie
★★★

**109** Pot-Bellied Pig
★★★

**113** Squirrel Monkey
★★★

**118** Cicada
★★★

**123** Tarantula
★★★

# Symbols

## Lines

— — — — — — — — —     Valley fold, fold in front.

—·—··—·—··—·—··—     Mountain fold, fold behind.

————————     Crease line.

·················     X-ray or guide line.

## Arrows

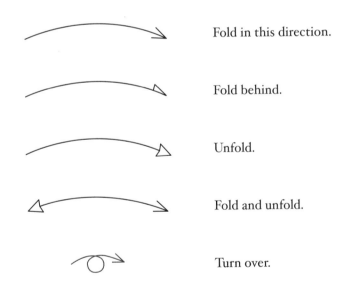

Fold in this direction.

Fold behind.

Unfold.

Fold and unfold.

Turn over.

Sink or three dimensional folding.

Place your finger between these layers.

# Basic Folds

### Pleat Fold.

Fold back and forth. Each pleat is composed of one valley and mountain fold. Here are two examples.

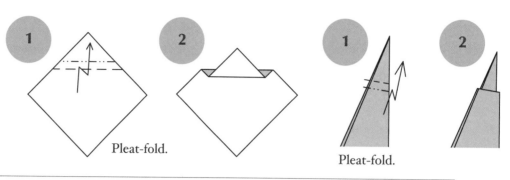

Pleat-fold.

Pleat-fold.

### Squash Fold.

In a squash fold, some paper is opened and then made flat. The shaded arrow shows where to place your finger.

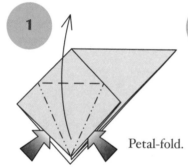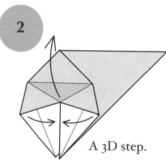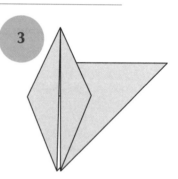

Squash-fold.

A 3D step.

### Petal Fold.

In a petal fold, one point is folded up while two opposite sides meet each other.

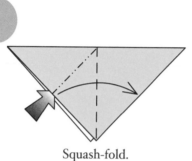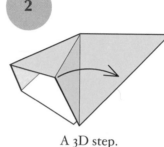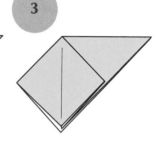

Petal-fold.

A 3D step.

### Rabbit Ear.

To fold a rabbit ear, one corner is folded in half and laid down to a side.

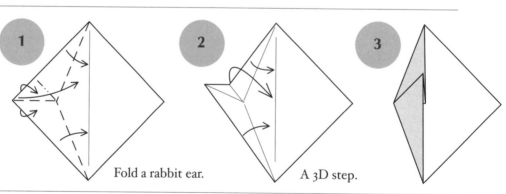

Fold a rabbit ear.

A 3D step.

### Double Rabbit Ear.

If you were to bend a straw you would be folding the double rabbit ear.

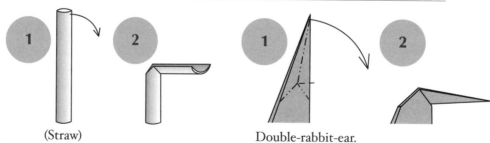

(Straw)

Double-rabbit-ear.

## Inside Reverse Fold.

In an inside reverse fold, some paper is folded between layers. Here are two examples.

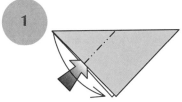
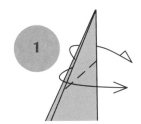

Reverse-fold.

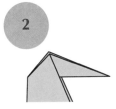
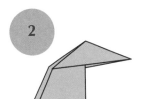

Reverse-fold.

## Outside Reverse Fold.

Much of the paper must be unfolded to make an outside reverse fold.

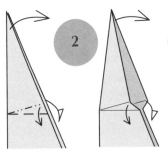

Outside-reverse-fold.

## Crimp Fold.

A crimp fold is a combination of two reverse folds. Open the model slightly to form the crimp evenly on each side. Here are two examples.

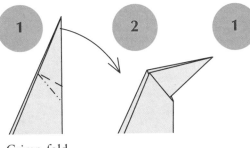

Crimp-fold.                    Crimp-fold.      A 3D step.

## Sink.

For a sink, some of the paper without edges is folded inside. To do this fold, much of the model must be unfolded.

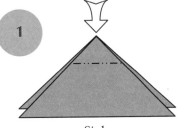
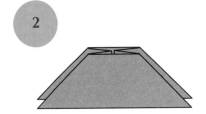

Sink.

## Spread Squash Fold.

A cross between a squash fold and sink fold, some paper in the center is spread apart and then made flat.

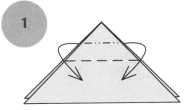
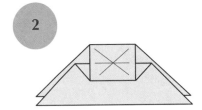

Spread-squash-fold.

## Preliminary Fold.

The Preliminary Fold is the starting point for many models. The maneuver in step 3 occurs in many other models.

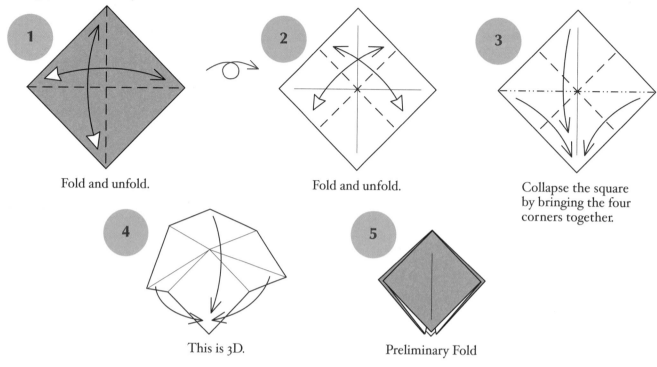

Fold and unfold.

Fold and unfold.

Collapse the square by bringing the four corners together.

This is 3D.

Preliminary Fold

## Bird Base.

Historically, the Bird Base has been a very popular starting point. The folds used in it occur in many models.

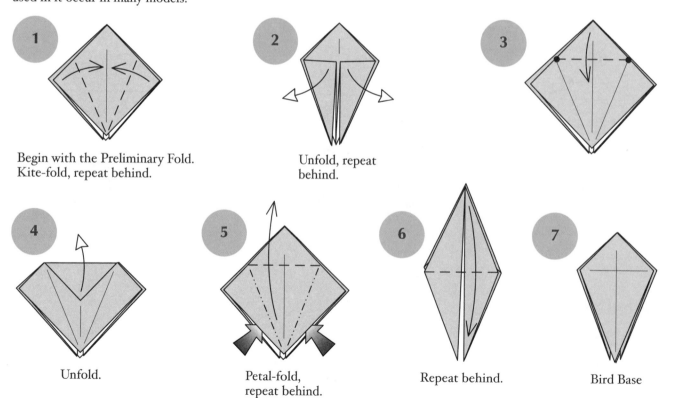

Begin with the Preliminary Fold. Kite-fold, repeat behind.

Unfold, repeat behind.

Unfold.

Petal-fold, repeat behind.

Repeat behind.

Bird Base

## Blintz Frog Base.

This uses the double unwrap fold which is shown in detail below.

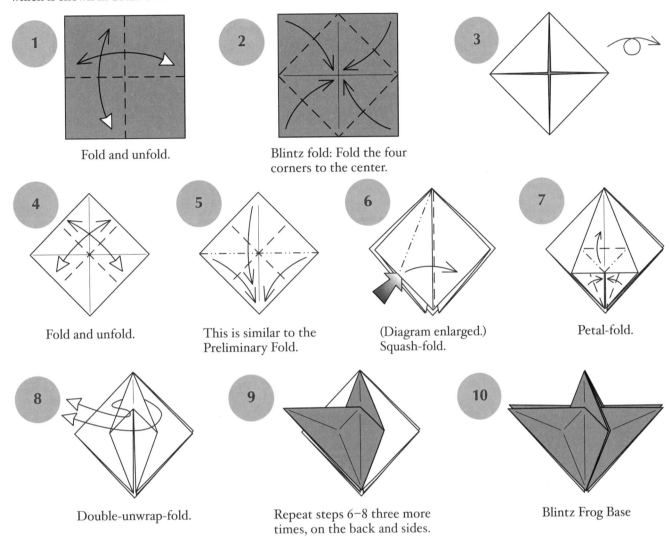

1  Fold and unfold.

2  Blintz fold: Fold the four corners to the center.

3

4  Fold and unfold.

5  This is similar to the Preliminary Fold.

6  (Diagram enlarged.) Squash-fold.

7  Petal-fold.

8  Double-unwrap-fold.

9  Repeat steps 6–8 three more times, on the back and sides.

10  Blintz Frog Base

## Double Unwrap Fold.

In the double unwrap fold, locked layers are unwrapped and refolded. Much of the folding is 3D. The diagrams are depicted as shown in steps 8 and 9 of the Blintz Frog Base.

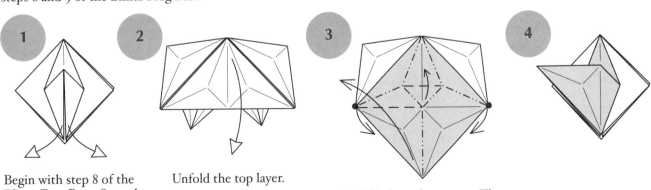

1  Begin with step 8 of the Blintz Frog Base. Spread at the bottom.

2  Unfold the top layer.

3  Refold along the creases. The dots will meet at the bottom.

4

# Appreciating Pets

Pets are wonderful for everybody. Children learn to take care of small animals and love to watch them grow. Older people benefit from selfless companionship offered by pets.

Ours is a symbiotic relationship. While pets get our care and protection, we enjoy their natural view of the world. Pets light up every time they see us. They let us know there is more to life than busy schedules and overuse of daily technology. Pet owners are known to have enriched lives.

Some pets have super powers. They hear sounds beyond ours, they fly, crawl through tiny spaces, and so much more. The eyes of many birds and turtles possess four cones (compared to our three) so they see colors beyond our experience and imagination. Cats and other mammals see fewer colors during the day but see far better than us at night. A dog's sense of smell is so much better than ours that we do not yet have technology to pick up the scents they detect. Many folk and mythological stories depict mice, birds, and other pets as the heroes who save the day by achieving feats not possible to humans.

Today there are pet stores, pet food, and many related products. But, long time ago, animals were not considered as pets. Around 12000 years ago, Asian wolves and people bonded. People found wolves to be helpful for hunting, herding, and protecting their property. In return, the wolves were well-fed and taken care of. These wolves became domesticated dogs. Then, 8000 years ago, cats were domesticated. They "took care" of mice and other small rodents on farms. Thus, dogs and cats were instrumental in improving civilization.

In the past few centuries, fish and birds became popular as pets. Then reptiles, amphibians, and other exotic pets became popular. In time, we learned that, while many young animals are cute, they do not make appropriate pets.

As we revel in their innocent company, pets show us compassion, sensitivity and intelligence beyond imagination. We may never wholly understand their world but we truly are fortunate to have them in our lives.

# Aquarium

Pet fish were enjoyed by the Egyptians, Romans, and Greeks. By the 10th century, the Chinese created the goldfish by breeding carp. But, the aquarium wasn't developed until the mid 19th century. Today we enjoy many variations of aquariums containing colorful fish, invertebrates, and plants.

## Clown Fish

The brightly-colored orange, white and black Clown Fish has become a favorite aquatic pet of children around the world and can be found in many school aquariums. Also known as an Anemonefish, the Clown Fish makes its home within the tentacles of sea anemones in the ocean, and is a salt-water fish.

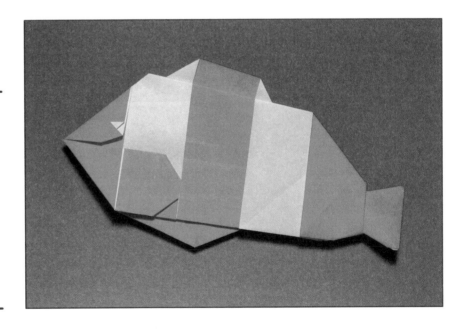

**1** Fold and unfold to find the 1/4 mark.

**2** Fold and unfold in the center.

**3** Fold and unfold in the center along the diagonal.

**4**

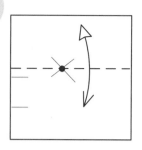

Fold and unfold.

**5**

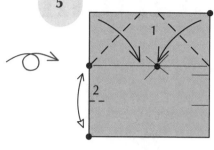

1. Fold to the line.
2. Fold and unfold on the edge.

**6**

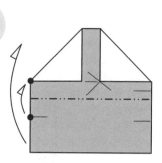

Mountain-fold so
the dots meet.

**7**

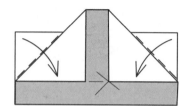

**8**

Fold up so the dots meet.

**9**

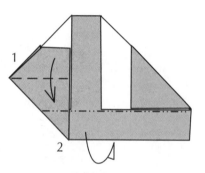

1. Fold down.
2. Fold behind.

**10**

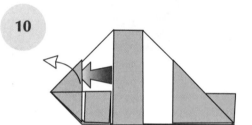

Pull out.

**11**

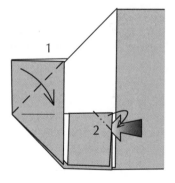

Part of the model is drawn.
1. Fold down.
2. Reverse-fold.

**12**

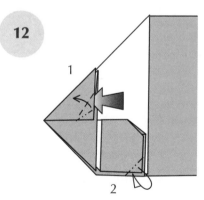

1. Squash-fold.
2. Fold behind.

**13**

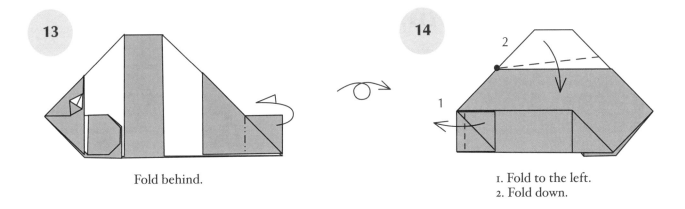

Fold behind.

**14**

1. Fold to the left.
2. Fold down.

**15**

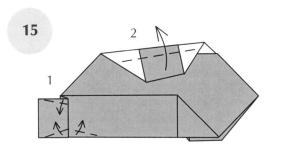

1. Shape the tail with small folds.
2. Fold up.

**16**

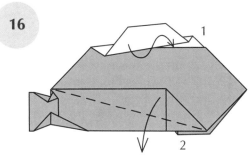

1. Tuck inside.
2. Fold down.

**17**

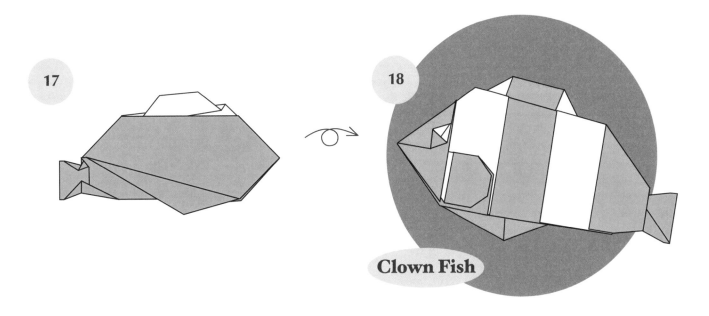

**18**

**Clown Fish**

# Simple Angelfish

Angelfish are members of the cichlid family that come from the Amazon and other rivers in South America. These beautiful freshwater fish can be found sporting a variety of spectacular colors and designs.

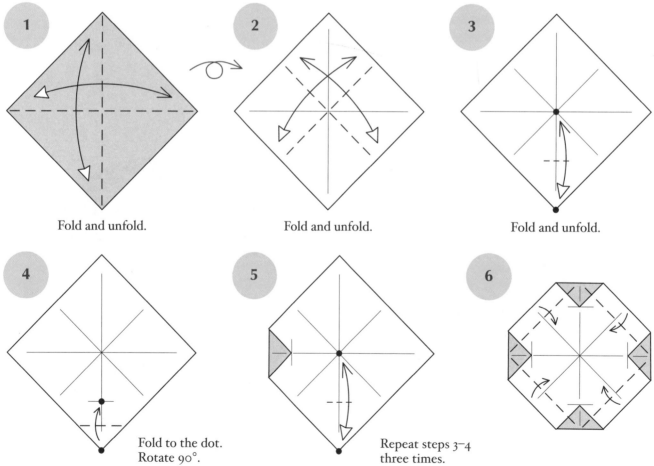

**1** Fold and unfold.

**2** Fold and unfold.

**3** Fold and unfold.

**4** Fold to the dot. Rotate 90°.

**5** Repeat steps 3–4 three times.

**6**

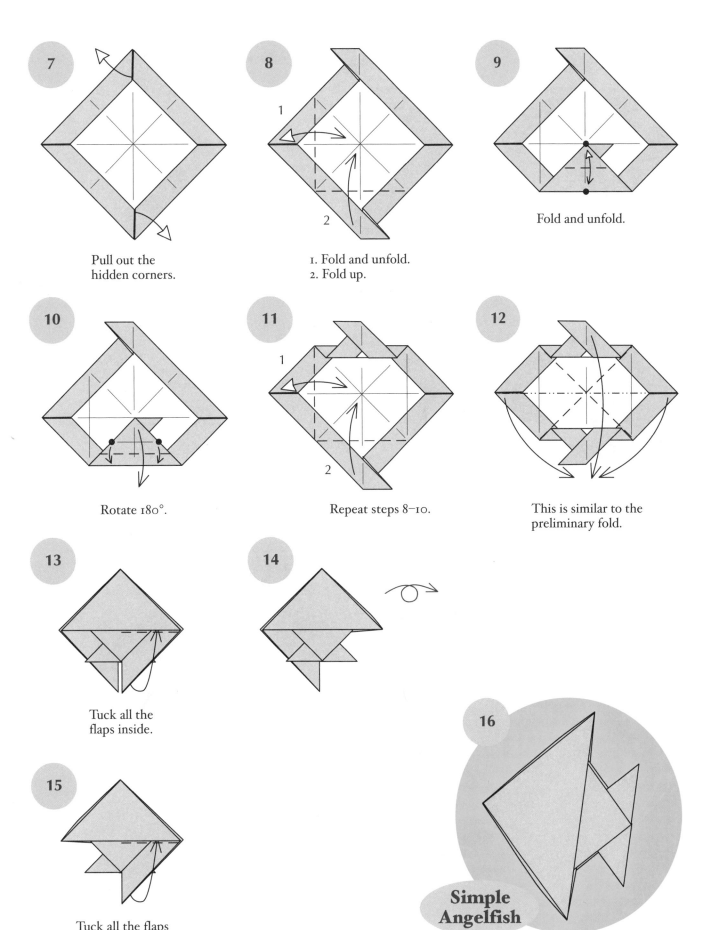

**7**

Pull out the
hidden corners.

**8**

1. Fold and unfold.
2. Fold up.

**9**

Fold and unfold.

**10**

Rotate 180°.

**11**

Repeat steps 8–10.

**12**

This is similar to the
preliminary fold.

**13**

Tuck all the
flaps inside.

**14**

**15**

Tuck all the flaps
inside. Rotate.

**16**

**Simple
Angelfish**

# Angelfish

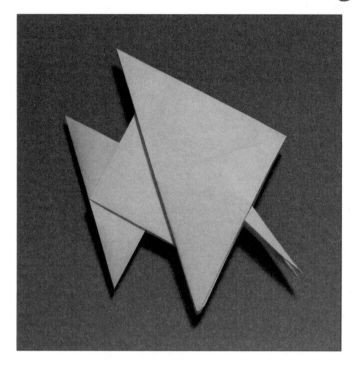

Angelfish are another favorite for freshwater aquariums, and sometimes sport long, flowing fins in addition to their bright colors. Large aquariums are better suited for them.

Begin with step 7 of the Simple Angelfish (page 18).

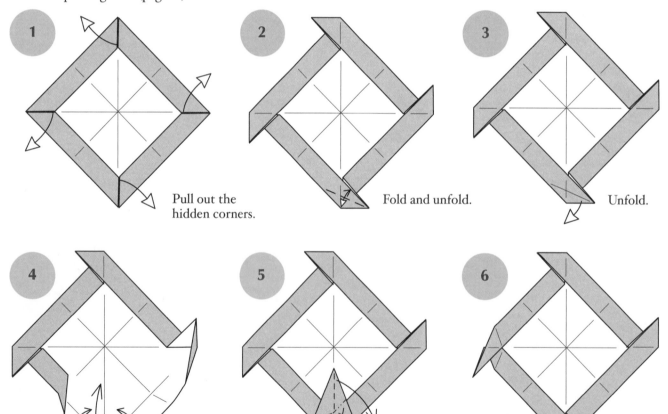

**1** Pull out the hidden corners.

**2** Fold and unfold.

**3** Unfold.

**4** Fold along some of the creases and flatten.

**5** Rabbit-ear. Rotate 90°.

**6** Repeat steps 2–5.

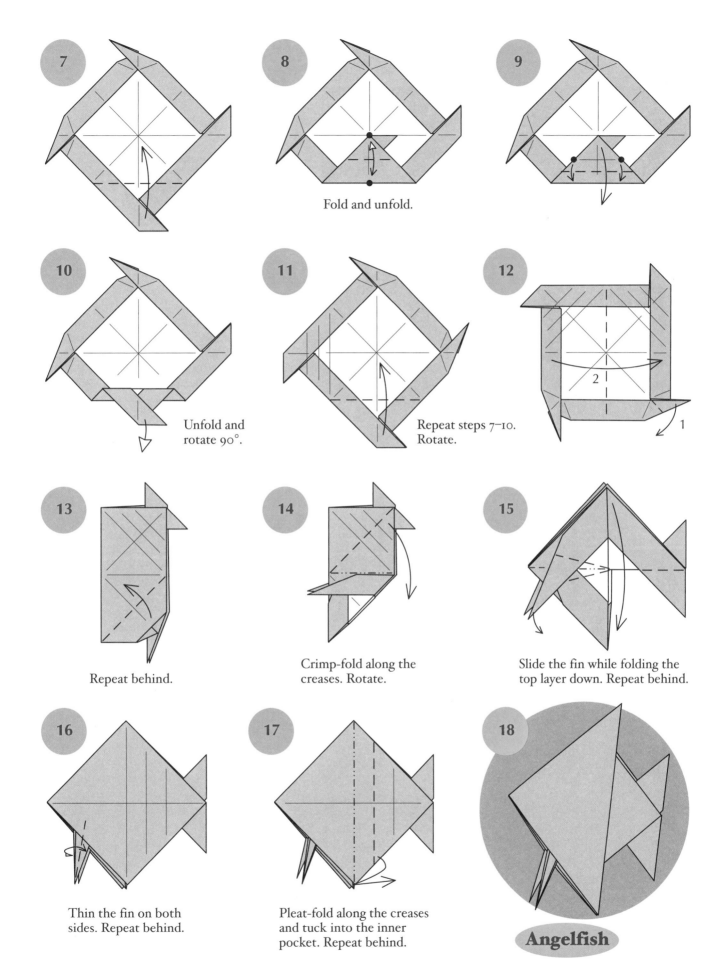

**7**

**8**

Fold and unfold.

**9**

**10**

Unfold and rotate 90°.

**11**

Repeat steps 7–10. Rotate.

**12**

2

1

**13**

Repeat behind.

**14**

Crimp-fold along the creases. Rotate.

**15**

Slide the fin while folding the top layer down. Repeat behind.

**16**

Thin the fin on both sides. Repeat behind.

**17**

Pleat-fold along the creases and tuck into the inner pocket. Repeat behind.

**18**

**Angelfish**

# Tropical Fish

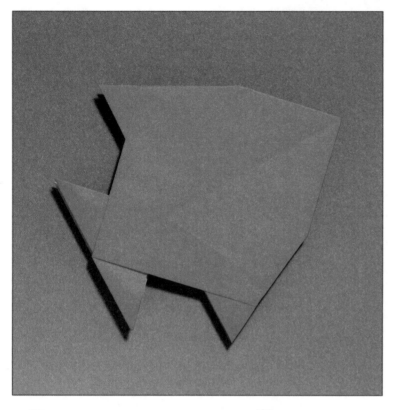

Tropical Fish is the label given to a wide variety of colorful and eye-pleasing fish that in the wild are generally found in tropical ocean areas. They can be both salt and freshwater depending on the specific fish, and make for an amazing array of pets in one's aquarium.

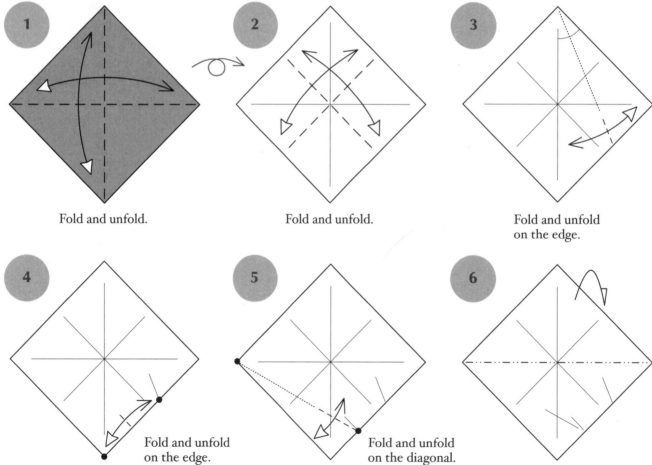

**1** Fold and unfold.

**2** Fold and unfold.

**3** Fold and unfold on the edge.

**4** Fold and unfold on the edge.

**5** Fold and unfold on the diagonal.

**6**

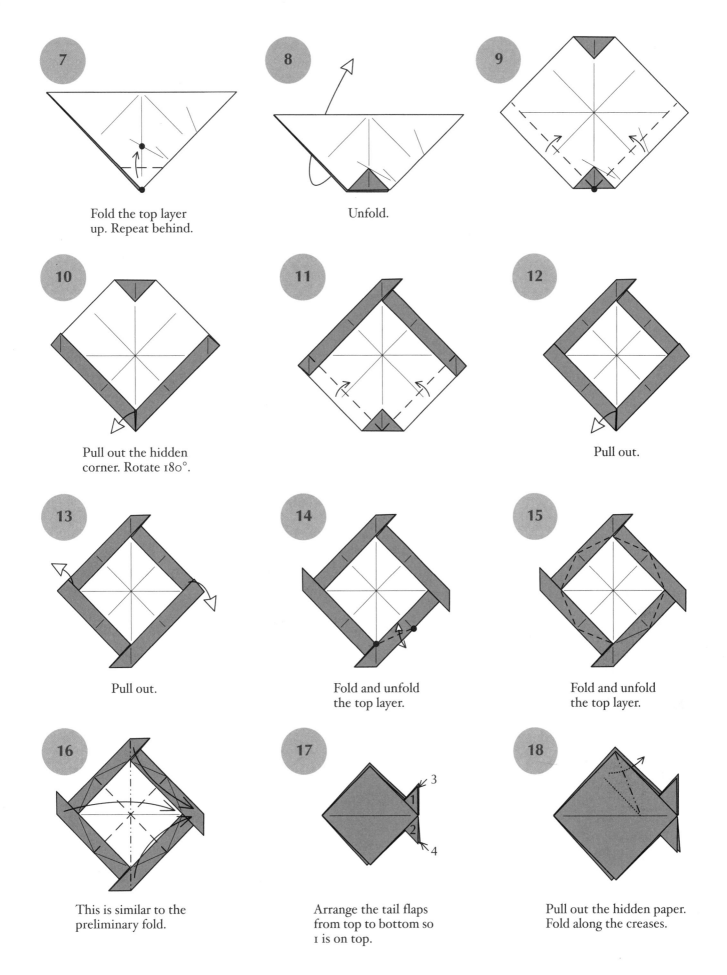

**7** Fold the top layer up. Repeat behind.

**8** Unfold.

**9**

**10** Pull out the hidden corner. Rotate 180°.

**11**

**12** Pull out.

**13** Pull out.

**14** Fold and unfold the top layer.

**15** Fold and unfold the top layer.

**16** This is similar to the preliminary fold.

**17** Arrange the tail flaps from top to bottom so 1 is on top.

**18** Pull out the hidden paper. Fold along the creases.

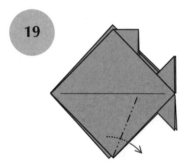

**19**

Repeat step 18 three times,
on the bottom and behind.

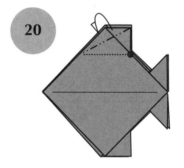

**20**

Mountain-fold. Use
the dot as a guide.

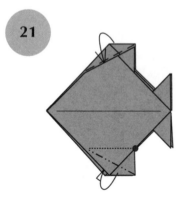

**21**

Repeat step 20 three times,
on the bottom and behind.

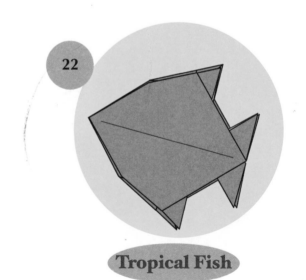

**22**

**Tropical Fish**

# Goldfish

Often chosen as a first pet, the typically orange Goldfish is an inexpensive yet fun pet to keep and take care of. Goldfish are frequently given as prizes at fairs and carnivals, and provide hours of fun as their owners watch them swim around their fishbowls and eat their fish food. Goldfish are freshwater fish.

**1**

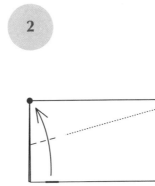

**2**

Fold the top layer so the edge meets the dot. Crease on the left.

**3**

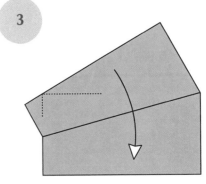

Unfold.

**4**

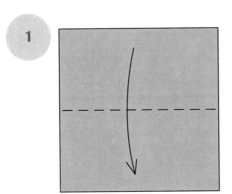

Fold the top layer. Repeat behind.

**5**

Unfold from behind. Rotate 90°.

**6**

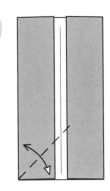

Fold and unfold.

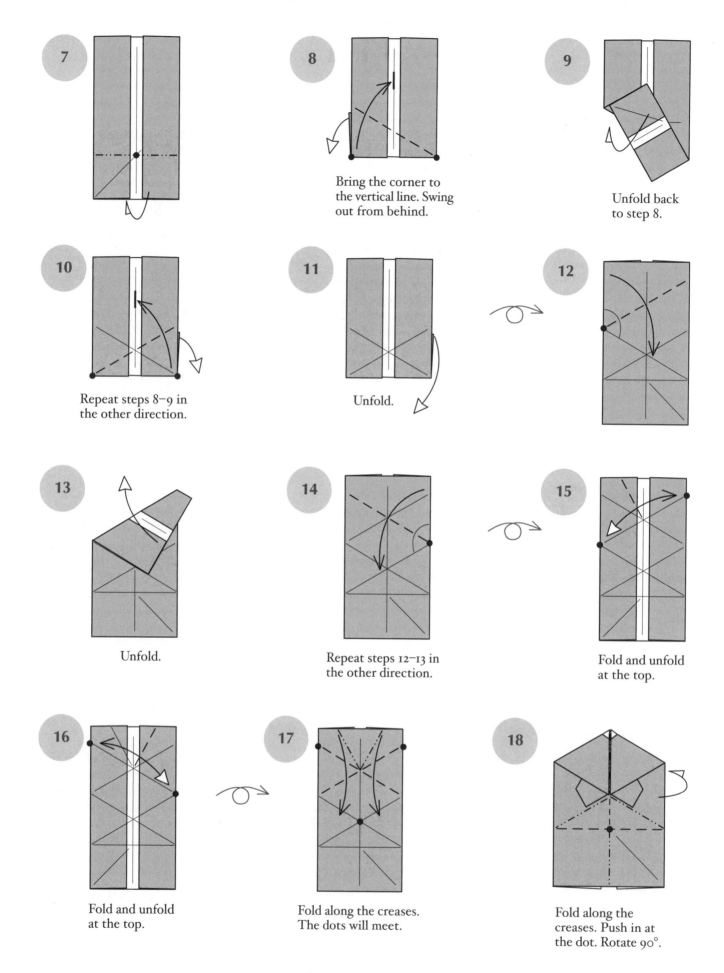

**7**

**8**

Bring the corner to the vertical line. Swing out from behind.

**9**

Unfold back to step 8.

**10**

Repeat steps 8–9 in the other direction.

**11**

Unfold.

**12**

**13**

Unfold.

**14**

Repeat steps 12–13 in the other direction.

**15**

Fold and unfold at the top.

**16**

Fold and unfold at the top.

**17**

Fold along the creases. The dots will meet.

**18**

Fold along the creases. Push in at the dot. Rotate 90°.

**19**

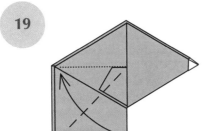

Fold all the layers.

**20**

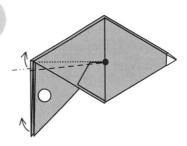

Pivot the tail by the dot in the center. Hold the tail at the white circle and slide it up.

**21**

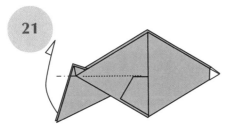

Mountain-fold
the inner layer.

**22**

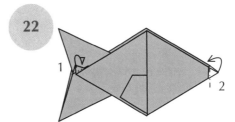

1. Mountain-fold, repeat behind.
2. Reverse-fold.

**23**

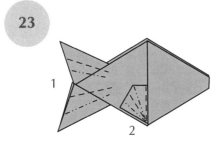

1. Pleat-fold the tail.
2. Pleat-fold the fins,
   repeat behind.

**24**

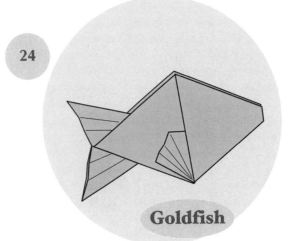

**Goldfish**

# Snail

While we're used to seeing the tiny snails on the rocks at the beach, some snails make wonderful pets. The larger land-based Garden Snail is a popular pet and many pet snails live for over a decade. They like to explore their surroundings and seem to enjoy the company of other snails.

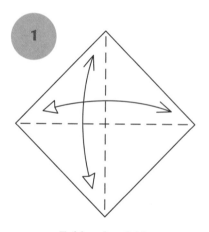

Fold and unfold.

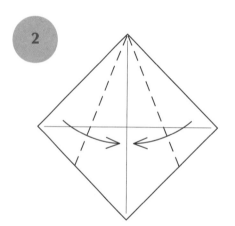

Kite-fold.

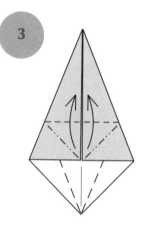

Squash folds.

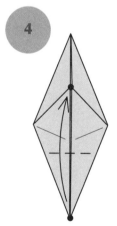

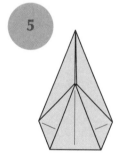

Rotate 180°.

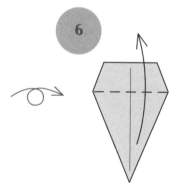

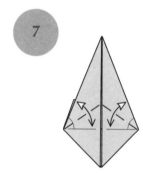

Fold and unfold.

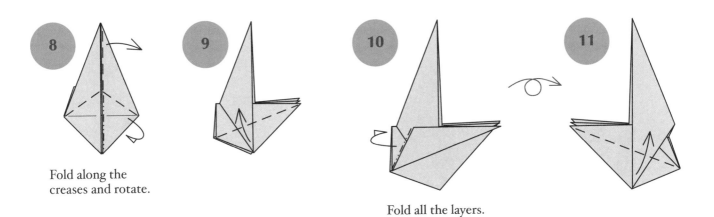

**8** Fold along the creases and rotate.

**9**

**10** Fold all the layers.

**11**

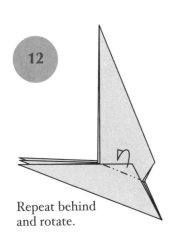

**12** Repeat behind and rotate.

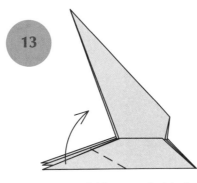

**13** Valley-fold, repeat behind.

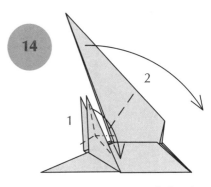

**14**
1. Rabbit-ear, repeat behind.
2. Valley-fold.

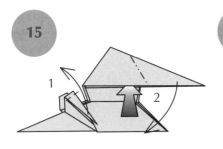

**15**
1. Valley-fold, repeat behind.
2. Reverse-fold.

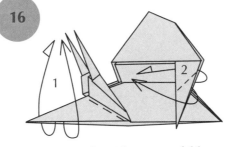

**16**
1. Outside-reverse-fold.
2. Outside-reverse-fold.

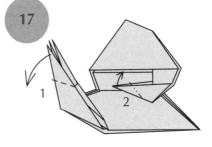

**17**
1. Outside-reverse-fold.
2. Reverse-fold.

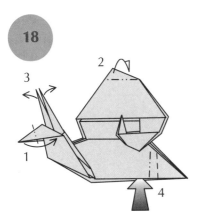

**18**
1. Reverse-fold.
2. Mountain-fold.
3. Spread the antennae.
4. Spread the bottom and make soft folds so the snail can stand.

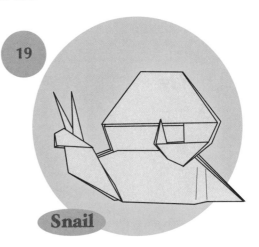

**19** **Snail**

# Seahorse

The Seahorse, named for its facial resemblance to a horse's head, has an exoskeleton and also has the interesting feature of the male carrying the fertilized eggs of its children in its own pouch, which many people mistake for the male giving birth, when in fact it is carrying the eggs after the female deposits them in the pouch. The Seahorse is a salt-water fish.

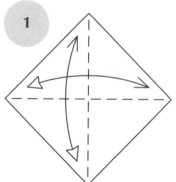

**1** Fold and unfold.

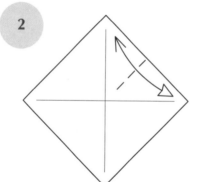

**2** Fold and unfold on the top.

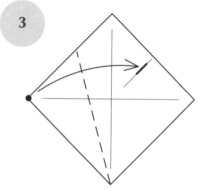

**3** Bring the corner to the line.

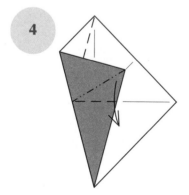

**4** Squash-fold.

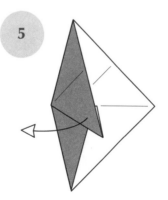

**5** Unfold.

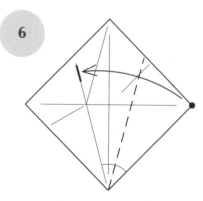

**6** Repeat steps 3–5 in the other direction.

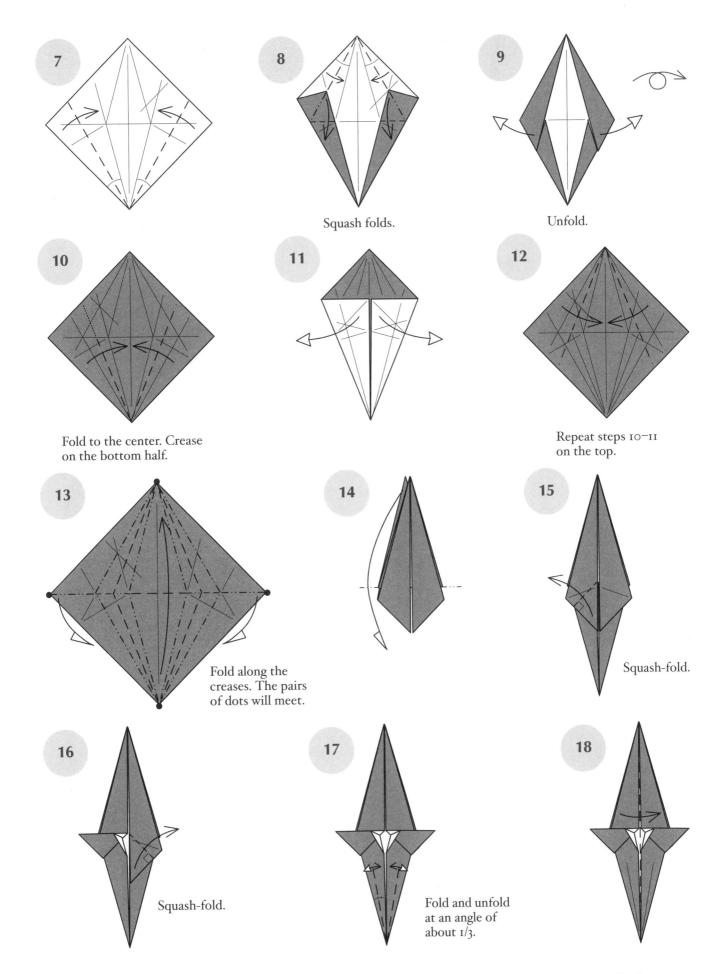

**7**

**8**

Squash folds.

**9**

Unfold.

**10**

Fold to the center. Crease on the bottom half.

**11**

**12**

Repeat steps 10–11 on the top.

**13**

Fold along the creases. The pairs of dots will meet.

**14**

**15**

Squash-fold.

**16**

Squash-fold.

**17**

Fold and unfold at an angle of about 1/3.

**18**

*Seahorse* 31

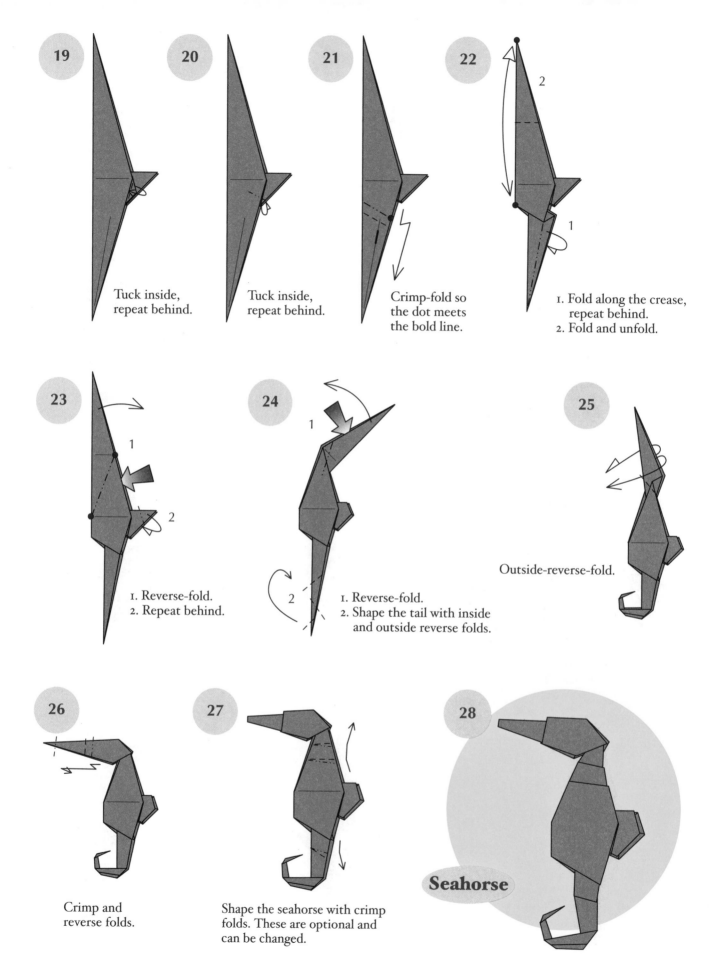

**19** Tuck inside, repeat behind.

**20** Tuck inside, repeat behind.

**21** Crimp-fold so the dot meets the bold line.

**22**
1. Fold along the crease, repeat behind.
2. Fold and unfold.

**23**
1. Reverse-fold.
2. Repeat behind.

**24**
1. Reverse-fold.
2. Shape the tail with inside and outside reverse folds.

**25** Outside-reverse-fold.

**26** Crimp and reverse folds.

**27** Shape the seahorse with crimp folds. These are optional and can be changed.

**28** Seahorse

# Reptiles & Amphibians

Pet reptiles and amphibians can be enjoyable but also challenging. Be careful not to choose one that can grow to be too large. With the right choice, these creatures can encourage children to learn more about nature. They are quiet and do not require much space. Reptiles and amphibians do not need as much care or attention as dogs and cats. While many are friendly and enjoy being handled, they are also content to be alone.

## Turtle

The turtle is a pet that takes its own house along with it wherever it goes, with its distinctive shell. Both aquatic and land Turtles are kept as pets, and while they are fun to keep, they do tend to require a lot of work and attention. When well taken care of, some Turtles can live in the range of 30 to 50 years, while some Tortoises can live for more than a century.

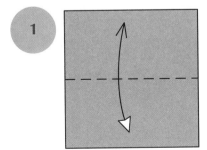

Fold and unfold.

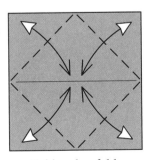

Fold and unfold.

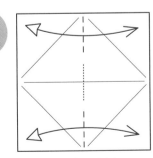

Fold and unfold on the top and bottom.

*Turtle* 33

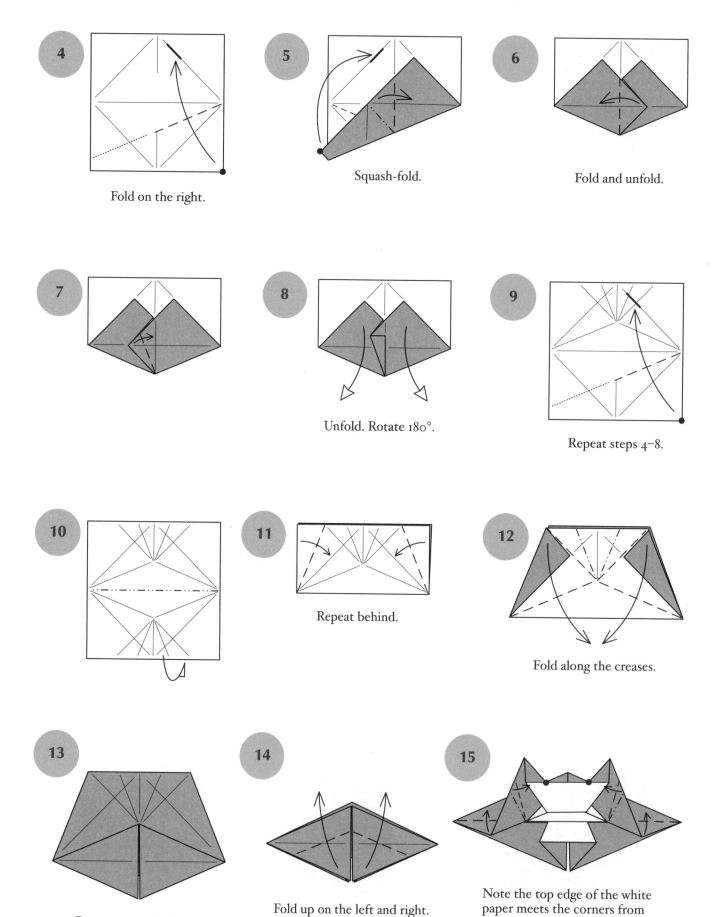

**4** Fold on the right.

**5** Squash-fold.

**6** Fold and unfold.

**7**

**8** Unfold. Rotate 180°.

**9** Repeat steps 4–8.

**10**

**11** Repeat behind.

**12** Fold along the creases.

**13** Repeat step 12 behind.

**14** Fold up on the left and right.

**15** Note the top edge of the white paper meets the corners from behind. Make squash folds on the left and right.

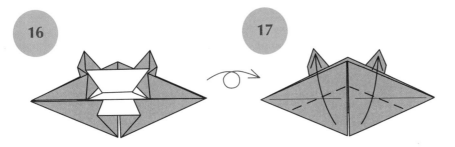

**16**

**17**

Repeat steps 14–15.

**18**

Unfold and rotate 90°.

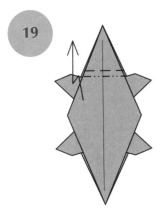

**19**

Pleat-fold

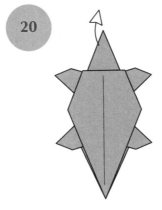

**20**

Unfold.

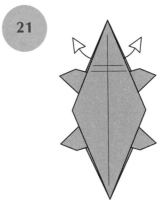

**21**

Spread.

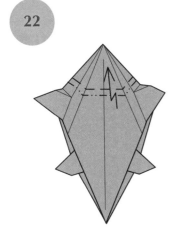

**22**

This is 3D. Fold along the creases.

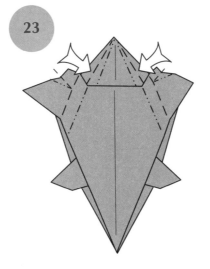

**23**

This is 3D. Flatten along the creases.

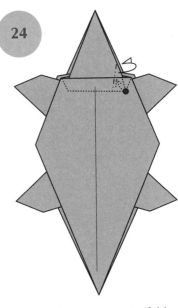

**24**

Spread some paper to fold the hidden corner at the dot, to the horizontal line.

*Turtle* 35

**25**

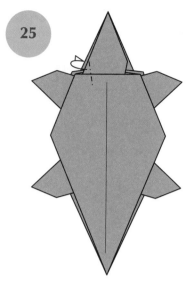

Repeat step 24
on the left.

**26**

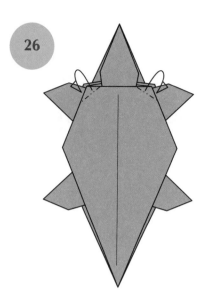

**27**

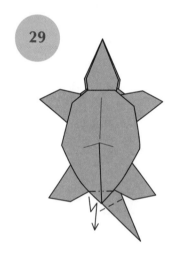

This is similar to
making squash folds.

**28**

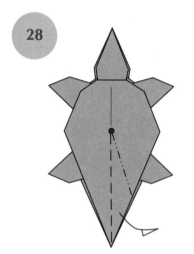

Puff out at the dot.

**29**

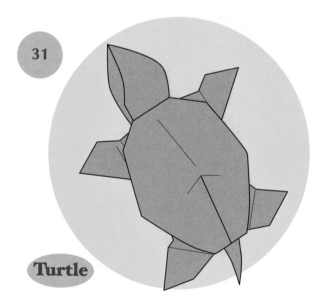

Pleat-fold.

**30**

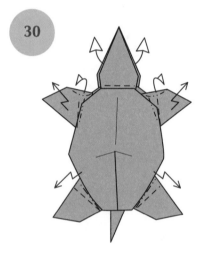

Lift the head up and spread
the layers to make it 3D.
Shape the legs.

**31**

**Turtle**

# Snake

All sorts of snakes are kept as pets, from the small Garter Snake to the large Python. Some snake owners present programs about snakes at schools and other organizations, while others simply keep their pet in the house like any other pet. Popular choices include the Corn Snake, Ball Python, and California Kingsnake.

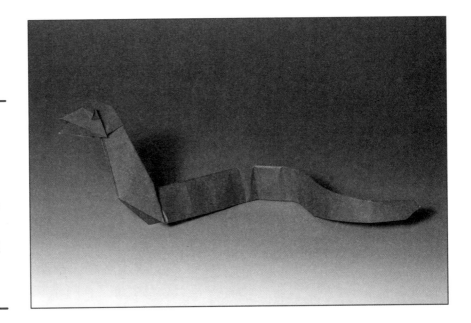

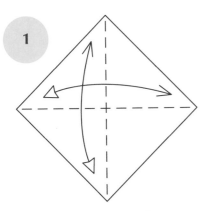

Fold and unfold.

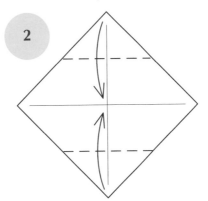

Fold to the center.

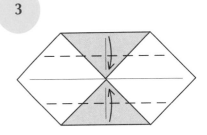

Fold to the center.

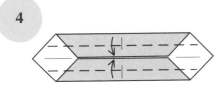

Fold to the center.

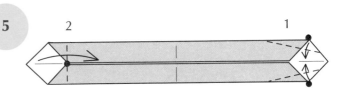

1. Bring the dots to the center.
2. Valley-fold.

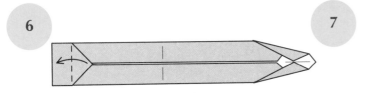

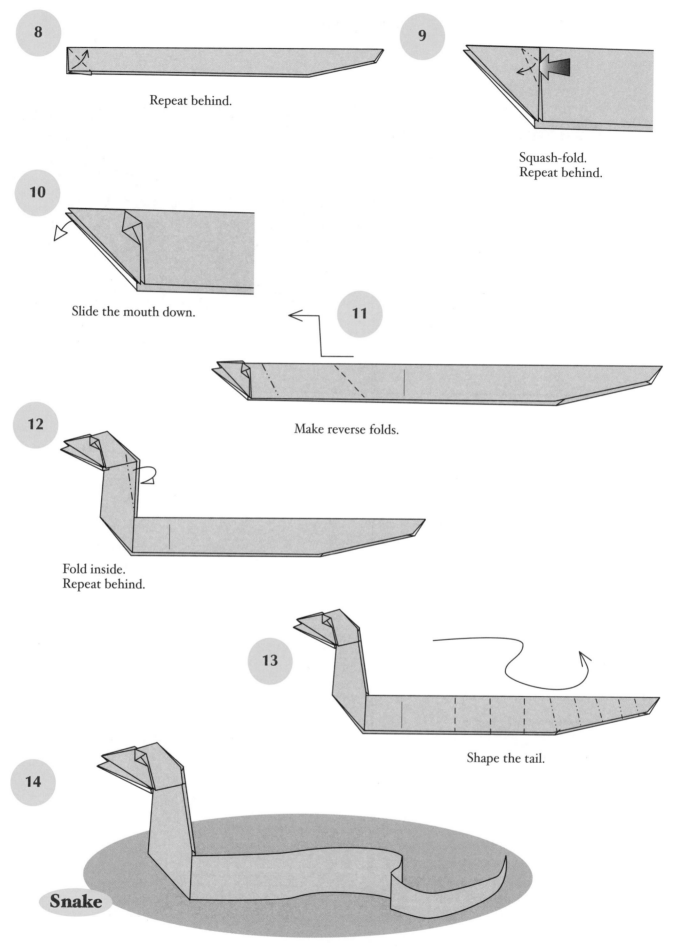

**8**

Repeat behind.

**9**

Squash-fold.
Repeat behind.

**10**

Slide the mouth down.

**11**

Make reverse folds.

**12**

Fold inside.
Repeat behind.

**13**

Shape the tail.

**14**

**Snake**

# Frog

A favorite pet at preschools, children love to follow the life cycle of a frog from tadpole to fully-grown frog. Some pet frog species can live for several decades, and there are many stories of parents who bought their young child a pet frog and are still taking care of the frogs after their children have grown up and left the house as adults.

**1**

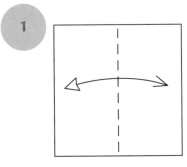

Fold and unfold.

**2**

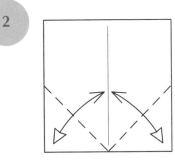

Fold and unfold.

**3**

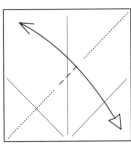

Fold and unfold in the center.

**4**

Bring the edge to the dot.

**5**

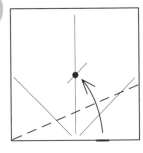

Unfold.

**6**

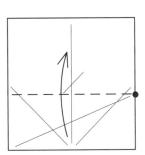

**7**

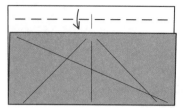

Rotate 180°.

**8**

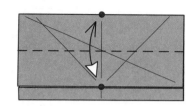

Fold and unfold
the top layer.

**9**

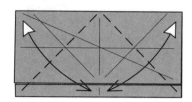

Fold and unfold
all the layers.

**10**

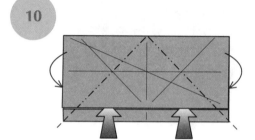

Reverse folds.

**11**

Petal-fold along
the creases.

**12**

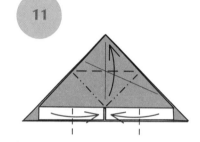

**13**

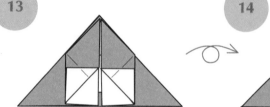

**14**

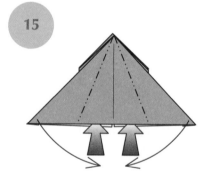

Fold to the center
and unfold.

**15**

Reverse folds.

**16**

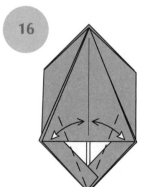

Fold to the center
and unfold.

**17**

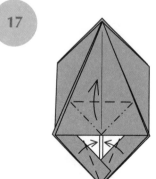

Petal-fold.

**18**

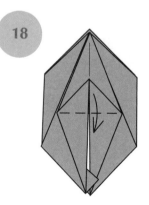

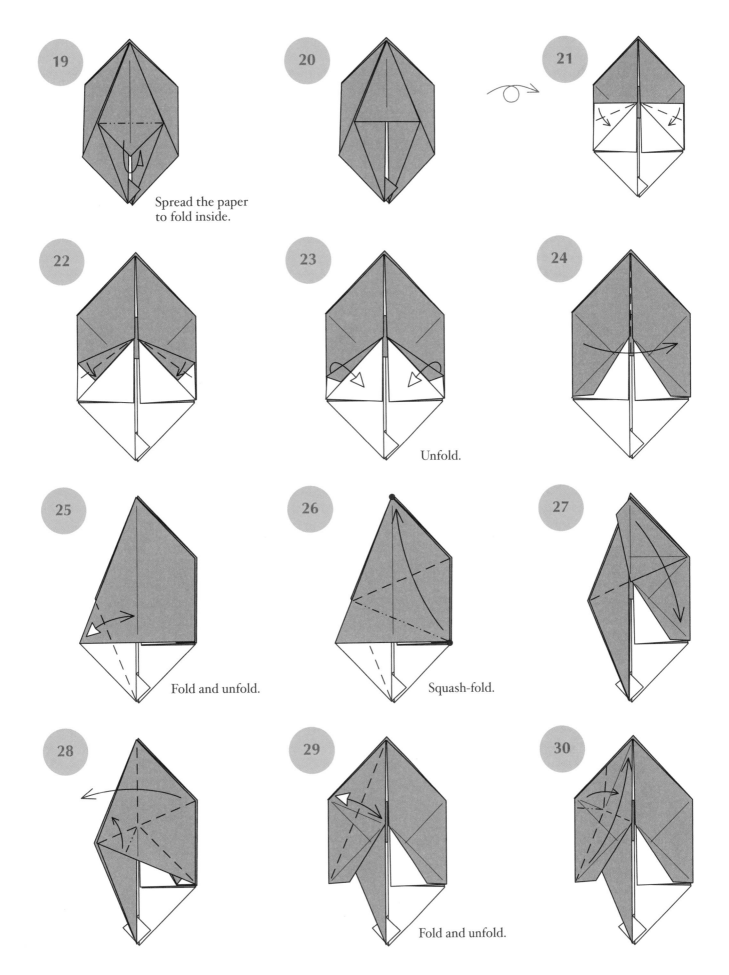

**19** Spread the paper to fold inside.

**20**

**21**

**22**

**23** Unfold.

**24**

**25** Fold and unfold.

**26** Squash-fold.

**27**

**28**

**29** Fold and unfold.

**30**

*Frog* 41

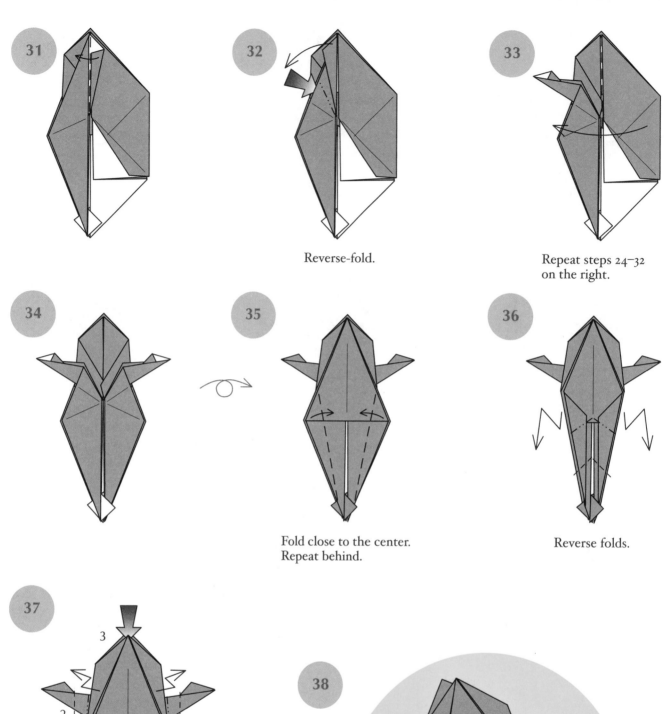

**31**

**32**

Reverse-fold.

**33**

Repeat steps 24–32
on the right.

**34**

**35**

Fold close to the center.
Repeat behind.

**36**

Reverse folds.

**37**

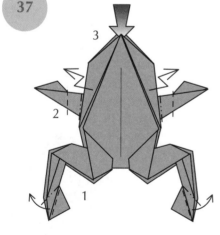

1. Reverse-fold.
2. Pleat-fold.
3. Open the mouth.

**38**

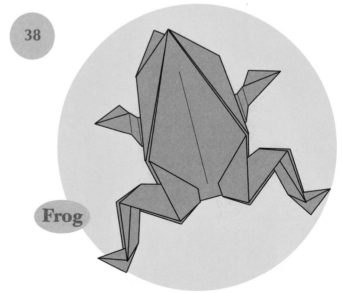

**Frog**

# Lizard

Lizards are fun to keep as pets, and come in a variety of colors and species. Geckos and Chameleons are among the popular lizards that are kept as pets.

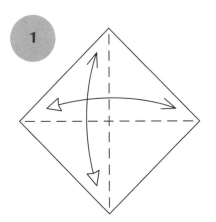

Fold and unfold.

Kite-fold and unfold.

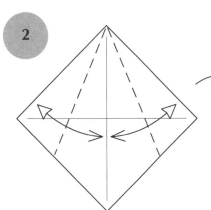

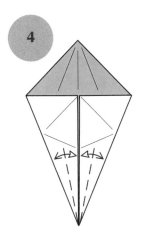

Fold and unfold the top layer.

Fold to the center and swing out from behind.

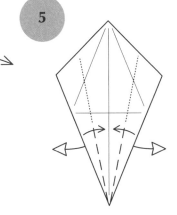

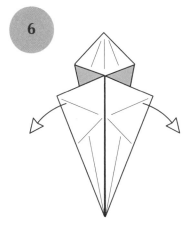

Unfold.

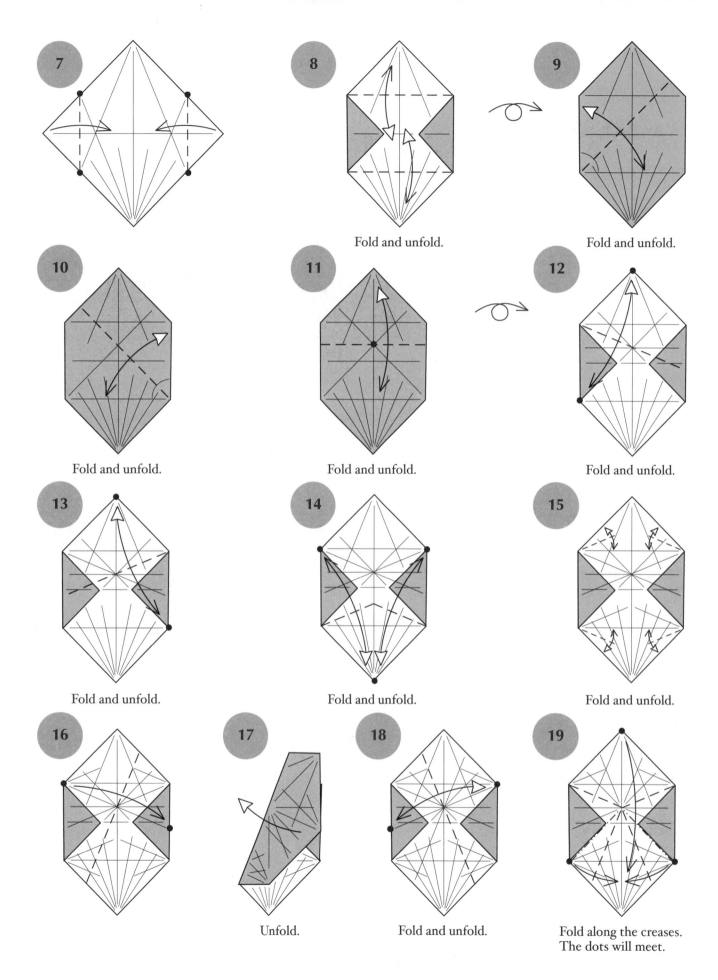

**7**

**8**

Fold and unfold.

**9**

Fold and unfold.

**10**

Fold and unfold.

**11**

Fold and unfold.

**12**

Fold and unfold.

**13**

Fold and unfold.

**14**

Fold and unfold.

**15**

Fold and unfold.

**16**

**17**

Unfold.

**18**

Fold and unfold.

**19**

Fold along the creases.
The dots will meet.

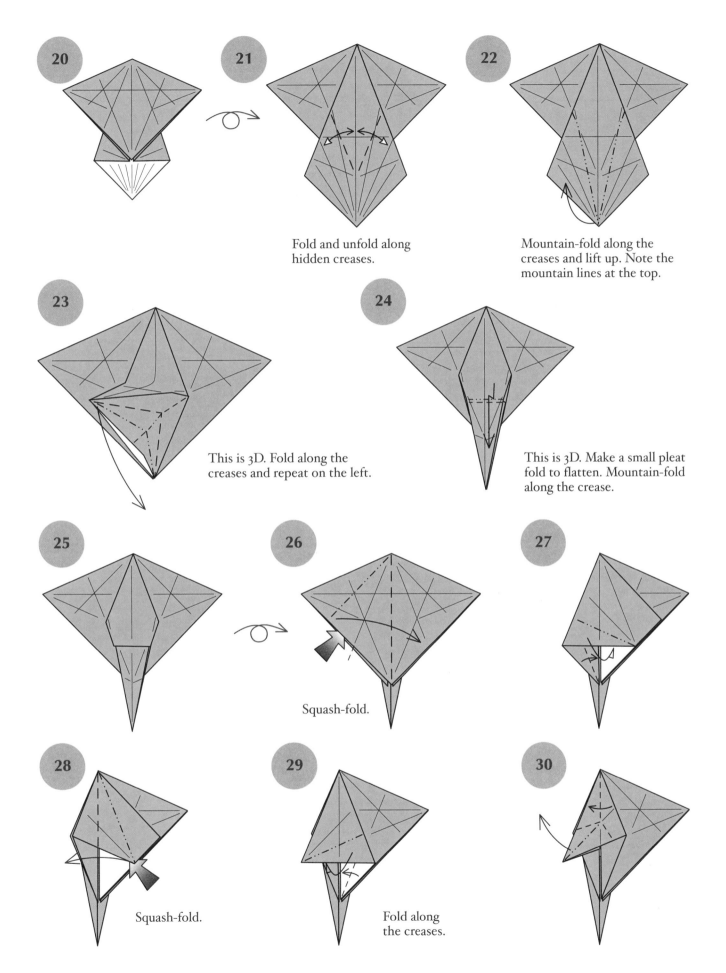

**20**

**21** Fold and unfold along hidden creases.

**22** Mountain-fold along the creases and lift up. Note the mountain lines at the top.

**23** This is 3D. Fold along the creases and repeat on the left.

**24** This is 3D. Make a small pleat fold to flatten. Mountain-fold along the crease.

**25**

**26** Squash-fold.

**27**

**28** Squash-fold.

**29** Fold along the creases.

**30**

*Lizard* 45

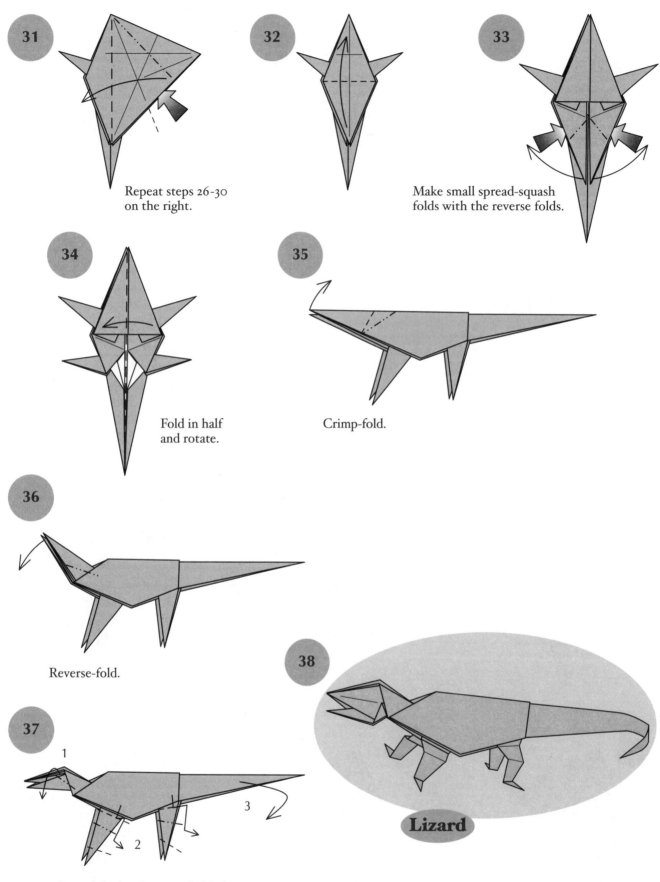

**31** Repeat steps 26-30 on the right.

**32**

**33** Make small spread-squash folds with the reverse folds.

**34** Fold in half and rotate.

**35** Crimp-fold.

**36** Reverse-fold.

**37**

1
2
3

1. Spread the head, repeat behind.
2. Pleat-fold the legs, repeat behind.
3. Curl the tail.

**38**

**Lizard**

# Birds

Pet birds liven up the home. Many pet birds do not adapt to the wild, they are happy to stay with people. They are incredibly smart and thrive on learning new tricks while occasionally copying their owners in surprising ways. These beautiful creatures are relatively easy to feed and can live long lives.

## Parrot

A favorite companion of pirates, Parrots come in a variety of colors and sizes. They are all physiologically capable of talking, using human speech in a voice that resembles the human voice, and this ability has made them uniquely popular as pets.

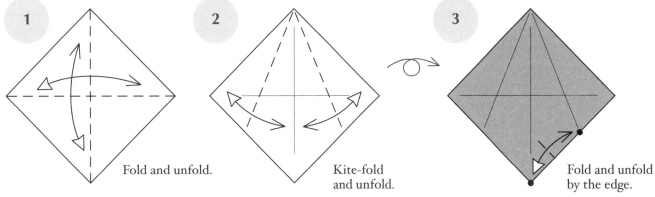

**1** Fold and unfold.

**2** Kite-fold and unfold.

**3** Fold and unfold by the edge.

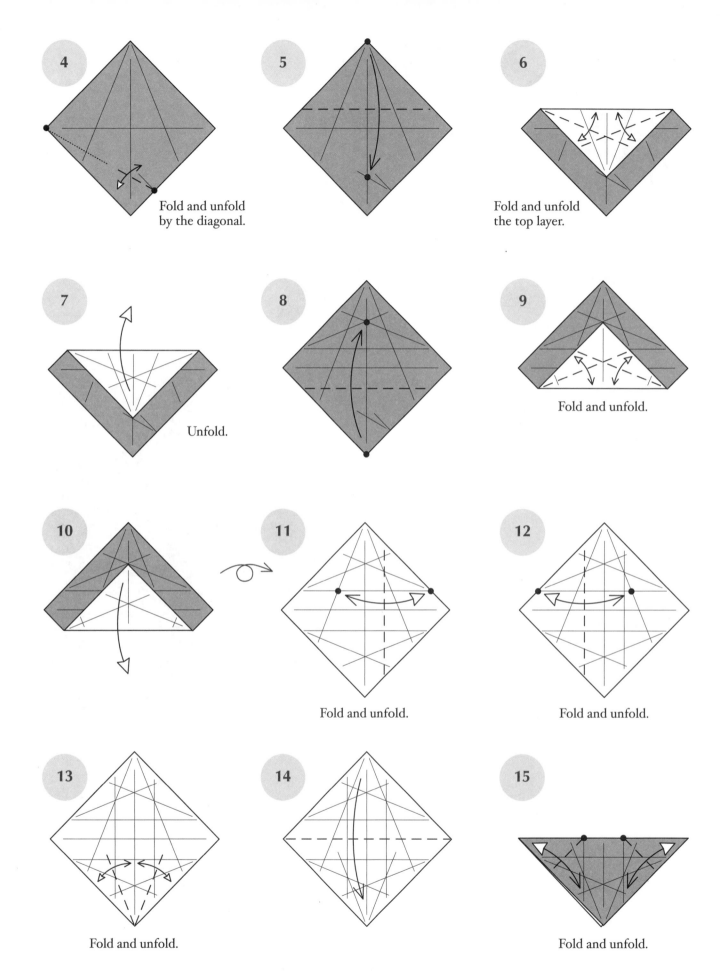

**4** Fold and unfold by the diagonal.

**5**

**6** Fold and unfold the top layer.

**7** Unfold.

**8**

**9** Fold and unfold.

**10**

**11** Fold and unfold.

**12** Fold and unfold.

**13** Fold and unfold.

**14**

**15** Fold and unfold.

**16**

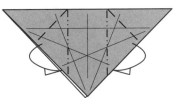

Crimp folds. Mountain-fold along the creases. The layers will overlap.

**17**

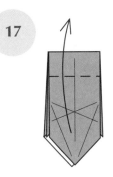

Fold along the crease.

**18**

The model is 3D. Flatten along some of the creases so the four dots form a diamond.

**19**

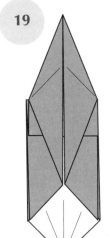

Repeat steps 17–18 behind.

**20**

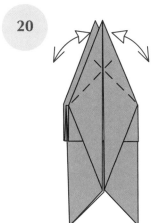

Fold and unfold along the creases.

**21**

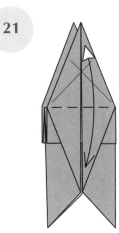

Fold and unfold.

**22**

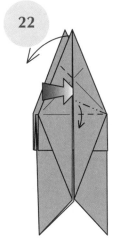

Squash-fold.

**23**

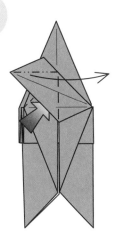

Squash-fold.

**24**

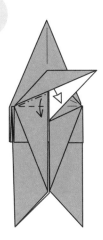

Pull out.

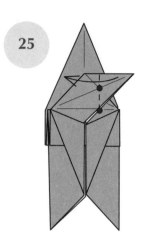

**25**

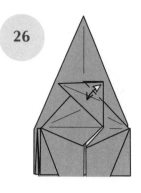

**26**

Fold and unfold.

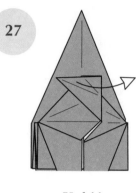

**27**

Unfold.

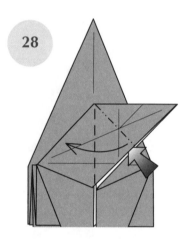

**28**

Squash-fold.

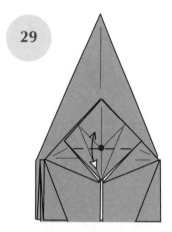

**29**

Fold and unfold.

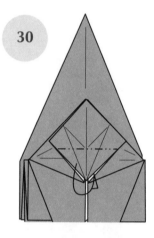

**30**

Fold along the crease.

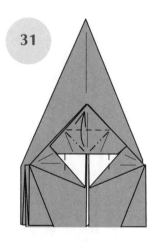

**31**

Petal-fold.

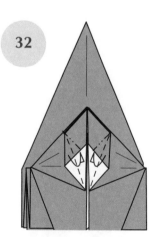

**32**

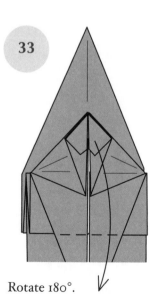

**33**

Rotate 180°.

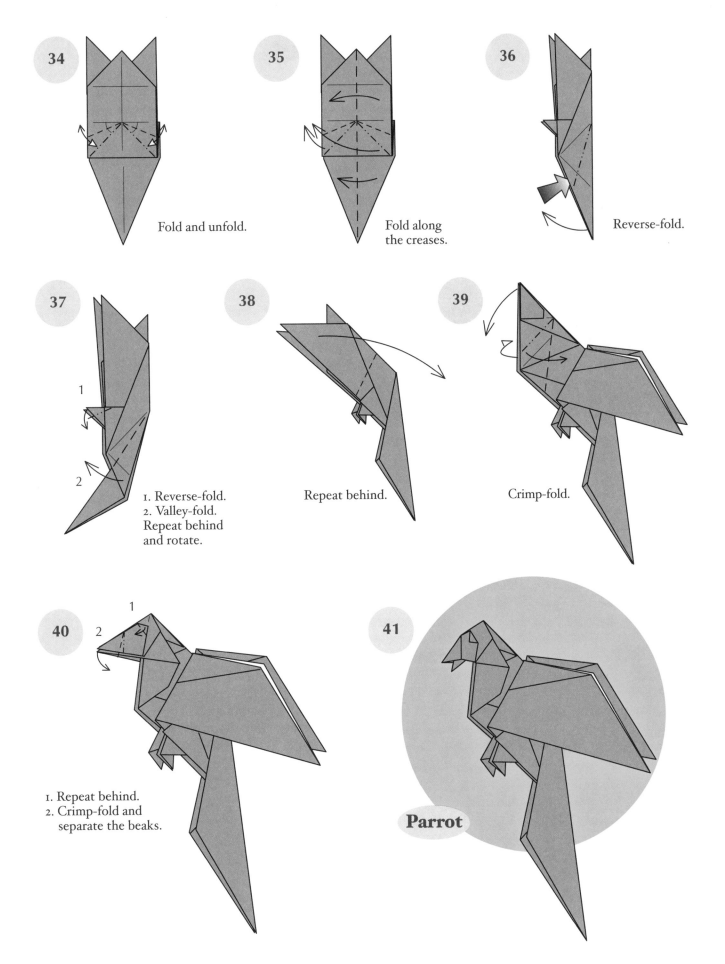

**34** Fold and unfold.

**35** Fold along the creases.

**36** Reverse-fold.

**37** 1. Reverse-fold.
2. Valley-fold.
Repeat behind and rotate.

**38** Repeat behind.

**39** Crimp-fold.

**40** 1. Repeat behind.
2. Crimp-fold and separate the beaks.

**41** **Parrot**

# Parakeet

The Parakeet, also known as a Budgie, is a very popular pet bird. Small and colorful, the Parakeet is a social bird and sings a bright trilling song.

**1**

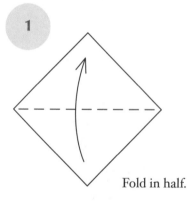

Fold in half.

**2**

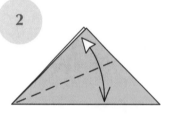

Fold and unfold the top layer.

**3**

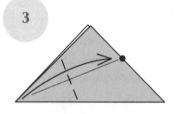

Fold the corner to the dot.

**4**

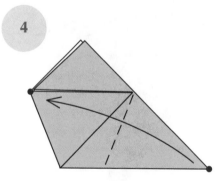

Fold the other corner.

**5**

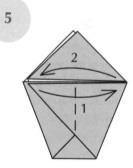

Fold on the left and right.

**6**

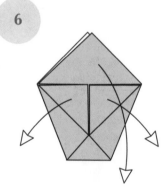

Unfold everything.

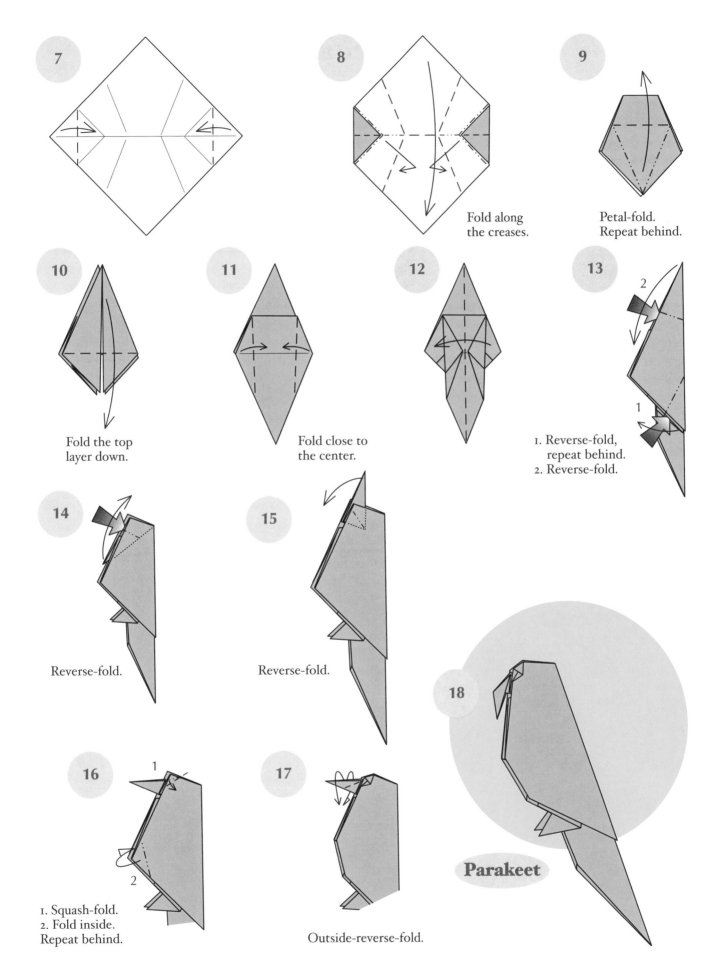

**7**

**8**

Fold along
the creases.

**9**

Petal-fold.
Repeat behind.

**10**

Fold the top
layer down.

**11**

Fold close to
the center.

**12**

**13**

1. Reverse-fold,
   repeat behind.
2. Reverse-fold.

**14**

Reverse-fold.

**15**

Reverse-fold.

**18**

**Parakeet**

**16**

1. Squash-fold.
2. Fold inside.
   Repeat behind.

**17**

Outside-reverse-fold.

# Cockatoo

With its distinctive crest, the Cockatoo is a large, active member of the Parrot family. Popular in tv shows and movies, there have even been viral videos of Cockatoos joyfully dancing to music.

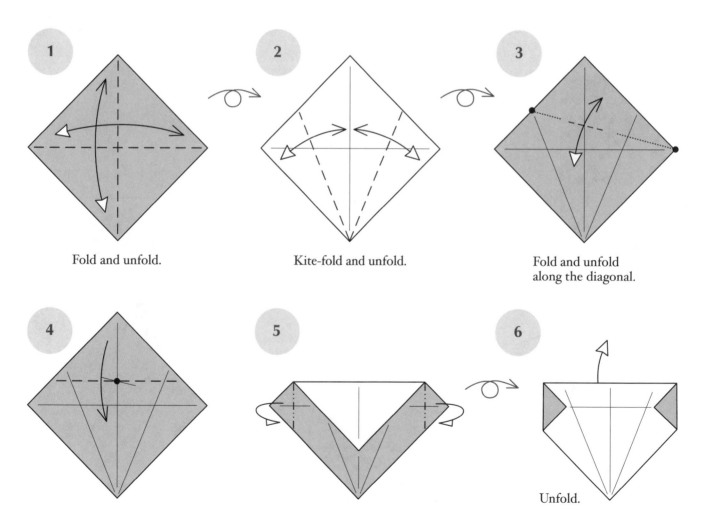

**1** Fold and unfold.

**2** Kite-fold and unfold.

**3** Fold and unfold along the diagonal.

**4**

**5**

**6** Unfold.

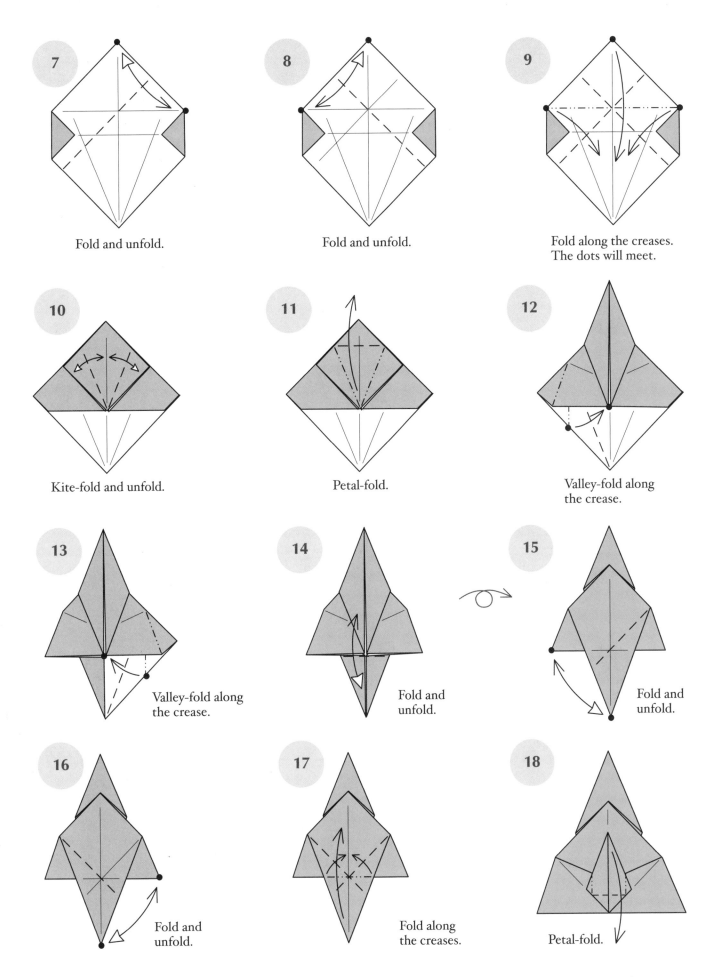

**7** Fold and unfold.

**8** Fold and unfold.

**9** Fold along the creases. The dots will meet.

**10** Kite-fold and unfold.

**11** Petal-fold.

**12** Valley-fold along the crease.

**13** Valley-fold along the crease.

**14** Fold and unfold.

**15** Fold and unfold.

**16** Fold and unfold.

**17** Fold along the creases.

**18** Petal-fold.

*Cockatoo* 55

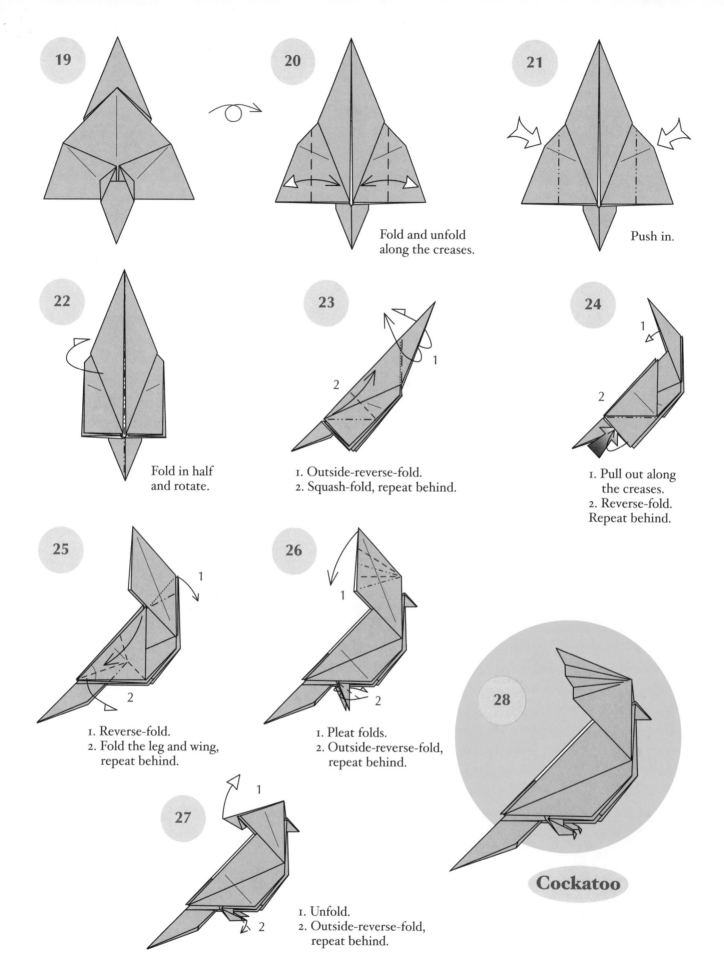

**19**

**20**

Fold and unfold
along the creases.

**21**

Push in.

**22**

Fold in half
and rotate.

**23**

1. Outside-reverse-fold.
2. Squash-fold, repeat behind.

**24**

1. Pull out along
the creases.
2. Reverse-fold.
Repeat behind.

**25**

1. Reverse-fold.
2. Fold the leg and wing,
repeat behind.

**26**

1. Pleat folds.
2. Outside-reverse-fold,
repeat behind.

**27**

1. Unfold.
2. Outside-reverse-fold,
repeat behind.

**28**

**Cockatoo**

# Canary

Often portrayed in cartoons as a small yellow bird, the Canary can also be found with orange, red or other-colored plumage. A popular pet, the canary can live for over 10 years.

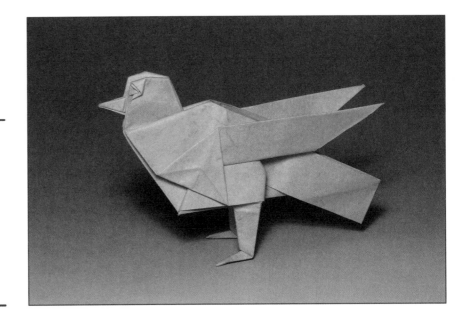

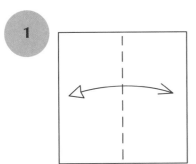

**1**

Fold and unfold.

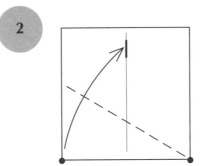

**2**

Bring the corner to the line.

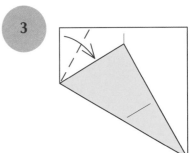

**3**

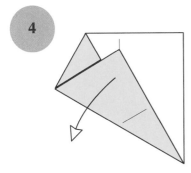

**4**

Unfold.

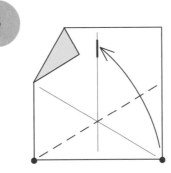

**5**

Repeat steps 2–4 in the other direction.

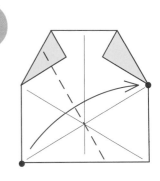

**6**

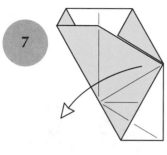

**7**

Unfold.

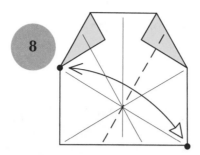

**8**

Fold and unfold.

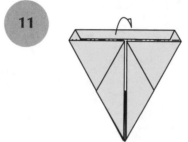

**9**

Fold along the creases.
The dots will meet.

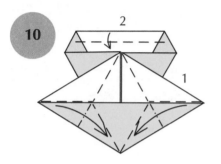

**10**

1. Make rabbit ears.
2. Fold down.

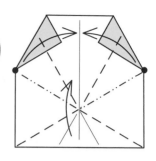

**11**

Fold behind.
Rotate 180°.

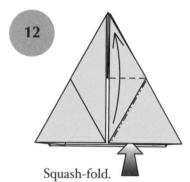

**12**

Squash-fold.

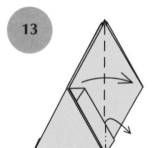

**13**

Spread at the bottom.

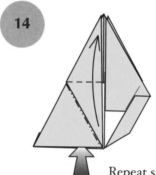

**14**

Repeat steps 12–13
on the left.

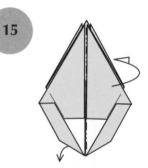

**15**

Fold in half and spread
at the bottom.

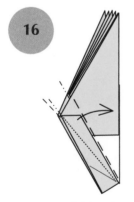

**16**

Crimp-fold. Valley-fold
along the crease.

**17**

Repeat behind.
Rotate.

**18**

Reverse-fold into
the second layer.

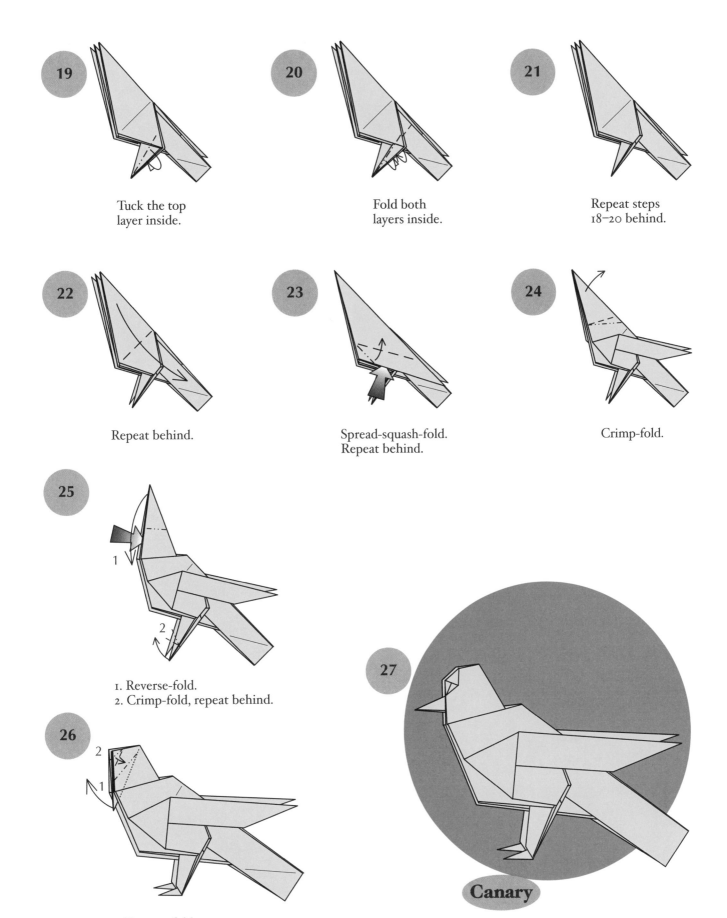

**19** Tuck the top layer inside.

**20** Fold both layers inside.

**21** Repeat steps 18–20 behind.

**22** Repeat behind.

**23** Spread-squash-fold. Repeat behind.

**24** Crimp-fold.

**25**
1. Reverse-fold.
2. Crimp-fold, repeat behind.

**26**
1. Reverse-fold.
2. Squash-fold, repeat behind.

**27** **Canary**

# Diamond Dove

Found in Australia, the Diamond Dove has both white and mottled grey feathers and distinctive orange eyes. Very adaptable to captivity, the Diamond Dove can form a great bond with its keeper.

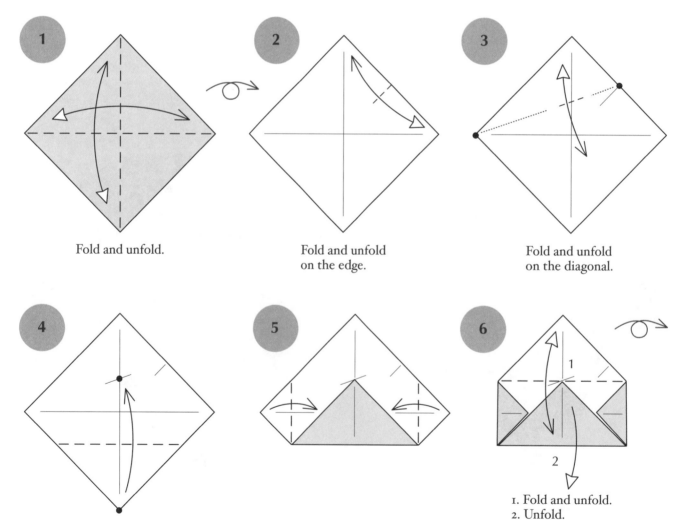

**1**

Fold and unfold.

**2**

Fold and unfold on the edge.

**3**

Fold and unfold on the diagonal.

**4**

**5**

**6**

1. Fold and unfold.
2. Unfold.

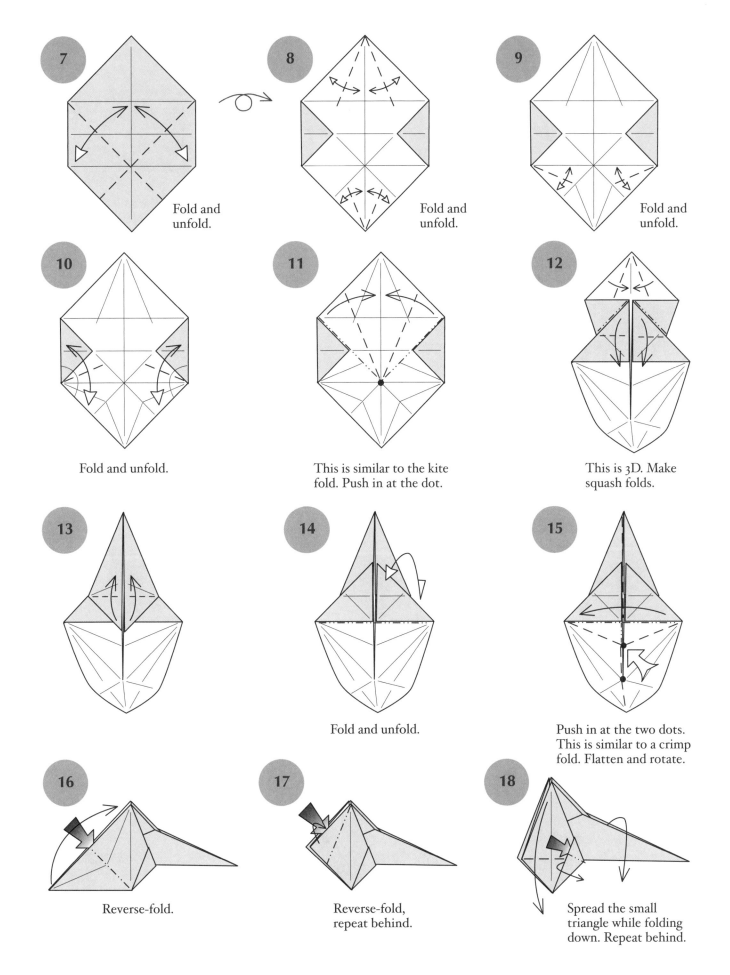

**7** Fold and unfold.

**8** Fold and unfold.

**9** Fold and unfold.

**10** Fold and unfold.

**11** This is similar to the kite fold. Push in at the dot.

**12** This is 3D. Make squash folds.

**13**

**14** Fold and unfold.

**15** Push in at the two dots. This is similar to a crimp fold. Flatten and rotate.

**16** Reverse-fold.

**17** Reverse-fold, repeat behind.

**18** Spread the small triangle while folding down. Repeat behind.

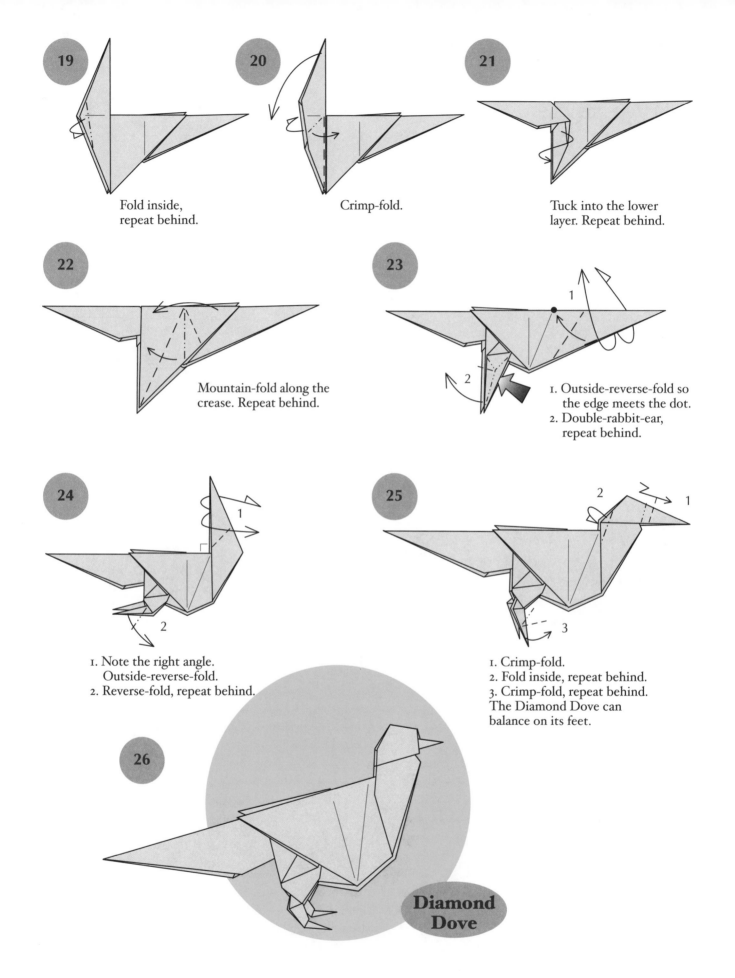

**19**

Fold inside,
repeat behind.

**20**

Crimp-fold.

**21**

Tuck into the lower
layer. Repeat behind.

**22**

Mountain-fold along the
crease. Repeat behind.

**23**

1. Outside-reverse-fold so
the edge meets the dot.
2. Double-rabbit-ear,
repeat behind.

**24**

1. Note the right angle.
Outside-reverse-fold.
2. Reverse-fold, repeat behind.

**25**

1. Crimp-fold.
2. Fold inside, repeat behind.
3. Crimp-fold, repeat behind.
The Diamond Dove can
balance on its feet.

**26**

**Diamond
Dove**

# Toucan

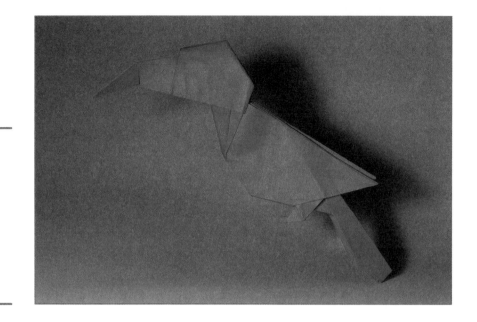

With its large, curved and often colorful bill that seems to make the rest of its body look small, the Toucan is found in tropical and sub-tropical areas of the world. Though it looks heavy, the bill is actually very light.

**1**

Fold and unfold.

**2**

Kite-fold and unfold.

**3**

Fold and unfold.

**4**

**5**

This is similar to a preliminary fold.

**6**

Petal-fold along the creases.

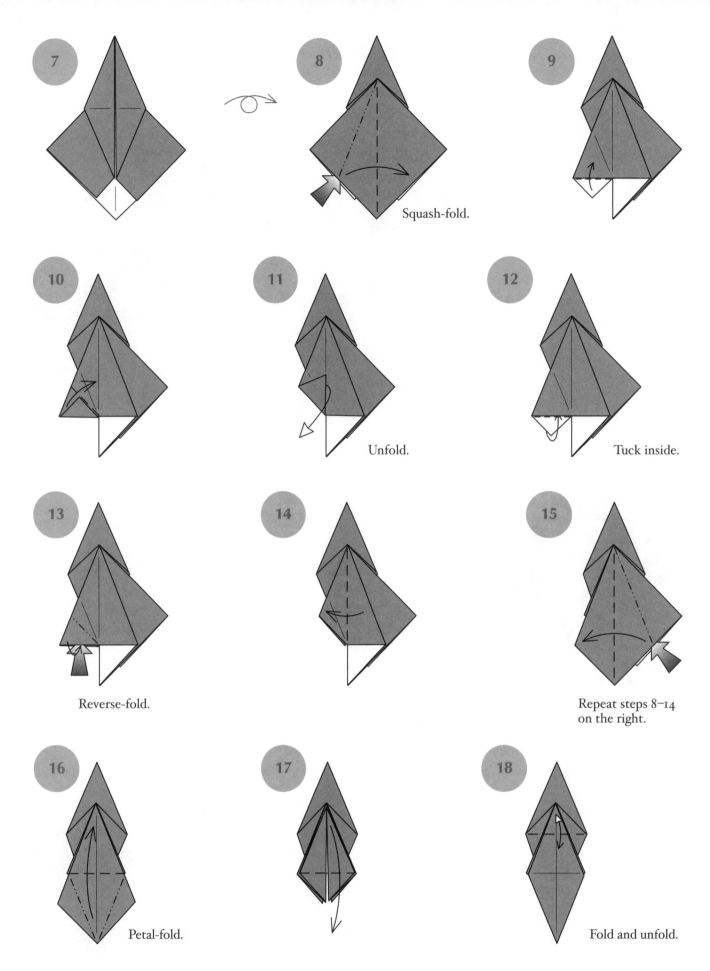

**7**

**8** Squash-fold.

**9**

**10**

**11** Unfold.

**12** Tuck inside.

**13** Reverse-fold.

**14**

**15** Repeat steps 8–14 on the right.

**16** Petal-fold.

**17**

**18** Fold and unfold.

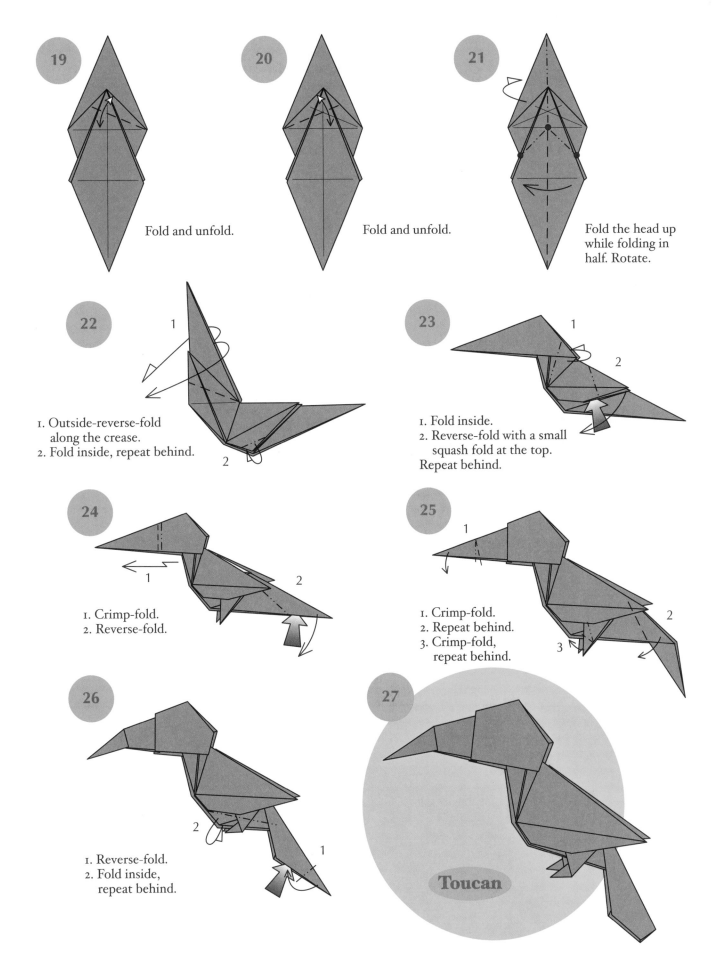

**19** Fold and unfold.

**20** Fold and unfold.

**21** Fold the head up while folding in half. Rotate.

**22**
1. Outside-reverse-fold along the crease.
2. Fold inside, repeat behind.

**23**
1. Fold inside.
2. Reverse-fold with a small squash fold at the top. Repeat behind.

**24**
1. Crimp-fold.
2. Reverse-fold.

**25**
1. Crimp-fold.
2. Repeat behind.
3. Crimp-fold, repeat behind.

**26**
1. Reverse-fold.
2. Fold inside, repeat behind.

**27** Toucan

# Mammals

Dogs, cats, and small mammals are the most popular pets. Many have been around for a long time and bred for their domestic qualities. Children enjoy playing with gerbils, mice, guinea pigs, and other pets. Dogs and cats have their special way of bonding to people. These pets are intelligent, inquisitive, enjoy toys, and are often loyal to their owners.

## Guinea Pig

A cute ball of fur with a humming voice, the Guinea Pig is a very popular pet with children and families. Many daycares have Guinea Pigs as pets to help teach the children about caring for animals. Guinea Pigs are relatively easy to take care of and bond well with people.

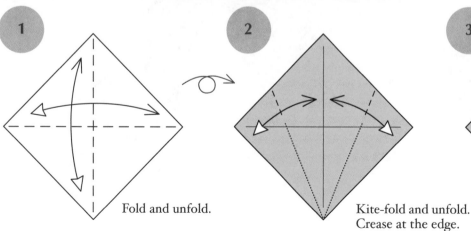

**1** Fold and unfold.

**2** Kite-fold and unfold. Crease at the edge.

**3**

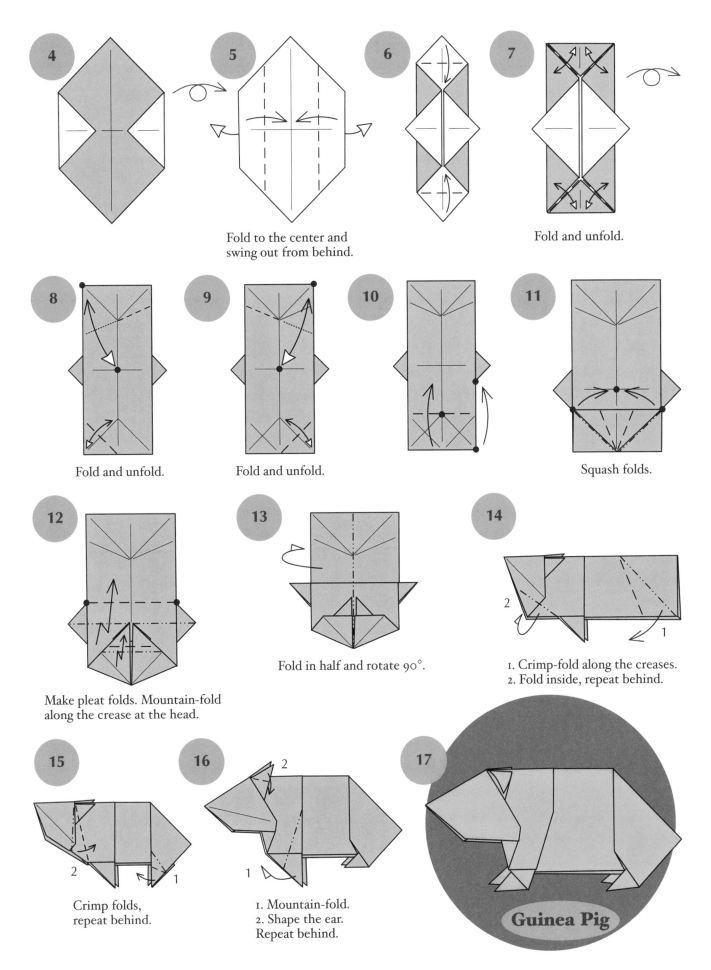

**4**

**5**

Fold to the center and
swing out from behind.

**6**

**7**

Fold and unfold.

**8**

Fold and unfold.

**9**

Fold and unfold.

**10**

**11**

Squash folds.

**12**

Make pleat folds. Mountain-fold
along the crease at the head.

**13**

Fold in half and rotate 90°.

**14**

1. Crimp-fold along the creases.
2. Fold inside, repeat behind.

**15**

Crimp folds,
repeat behind.

**16**

1. Mountain-fold.
2. Shape the ear.
Repeat behind.

**17**

**Guinea Pig**

# Hamster

The Hamster is a relative of the Mouse and can be quite clever. Also popular pets for families, many Hamsters can be taught tricks.

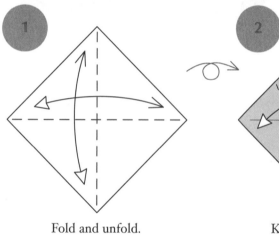

Fold and unfold.

Kite-fold and unfold.
Crease at the edge.

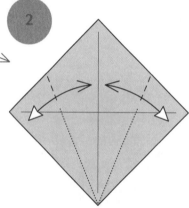

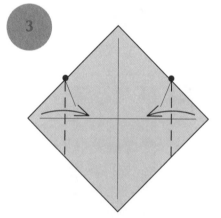

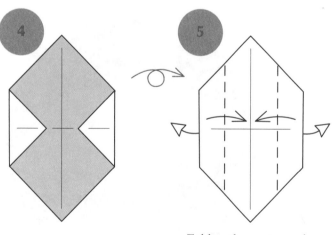

Fold to the center and
swing out from behind.

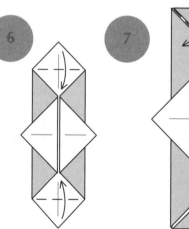

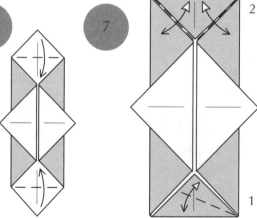

1. Fold and unfold.
2. Fold and unfold.

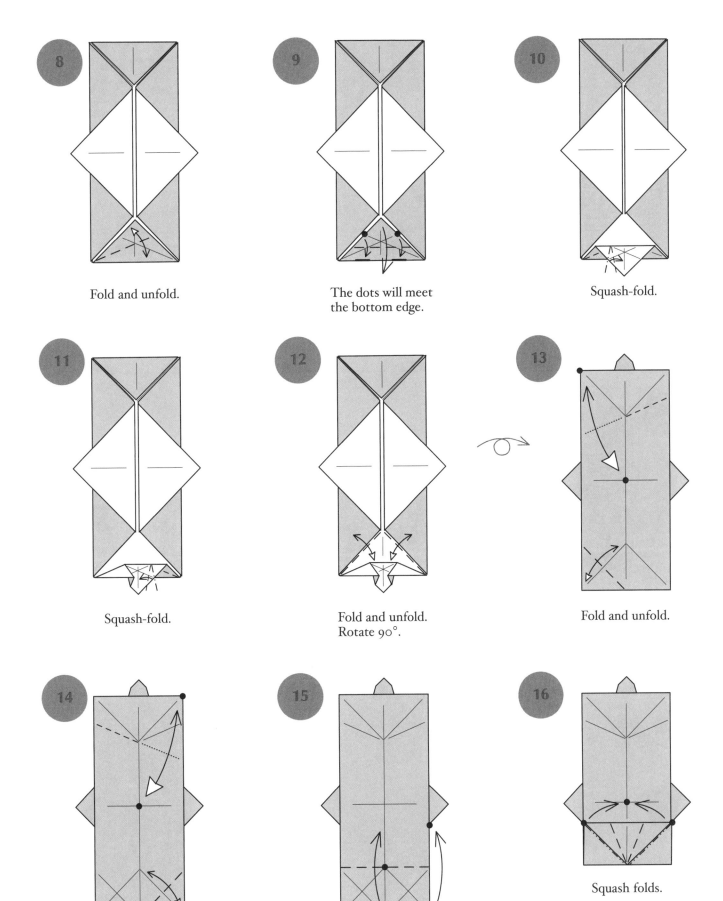

**8** Fold and unfold.

**9** The dots will meet the bottom edge.

**10** Squash-fold.

**11** Squash-fold.

**12** Fold and unfold. Rotate 90°.

**13** Fold and unfold.

**14** Fold and unfold.

**15**

**16** Squash folds.

*Hamster* 69

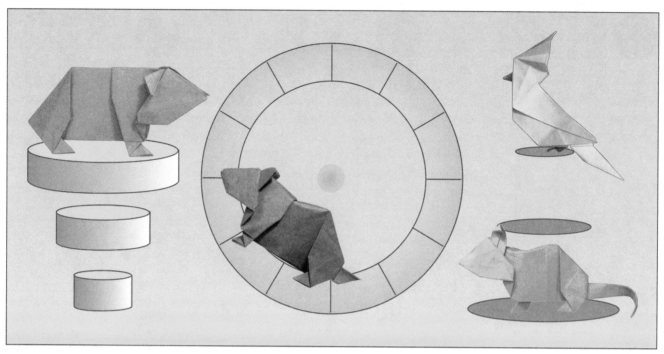

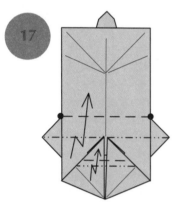

**17**

Make pleat folds. Mountain-fold along the crease at the head.

**18**

Fold in half and rotate 90°.

**19**

1. Crimp-fold along the creases.
2. Fold inside, repeat behind.

**20**

Crimp folds, repeat behind.

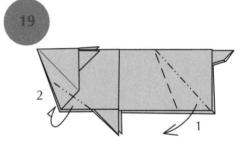

**22**

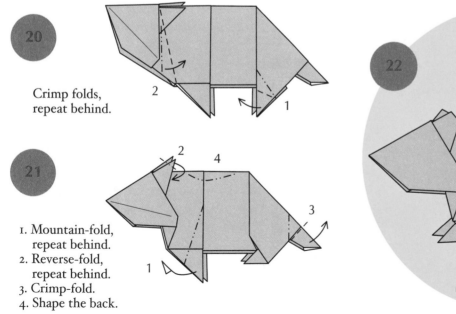

Hamster

**21**

1. Mountain-fold, repeat behind.
2. Reverse-fold, repeat behind.
3. Crimp-fold.
4. Shape the back.

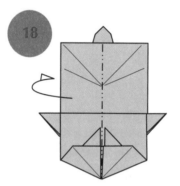

# Chinchilla

Chinchillas are in the rodent family and resemble squirrels but have much smaller tails. From the mountains of South America, Chinchillas have very soft fur and are quite mild-mannered. They are curious and friendly and do not require as much care as other pets.

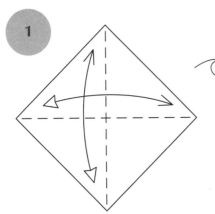

**1**

Fold and unfold.

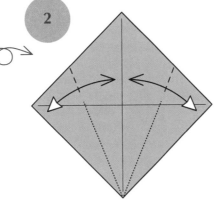

**2**

Fold and unfold.

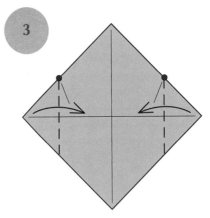

**3**

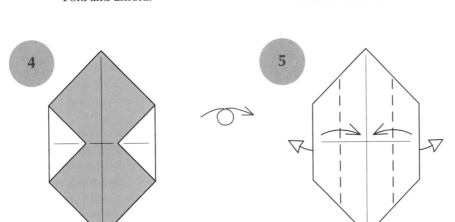

**4**

**5**

Fold to the center and swing out from behind.

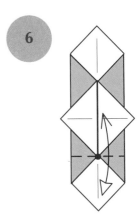

**6**

Fold and unfold.

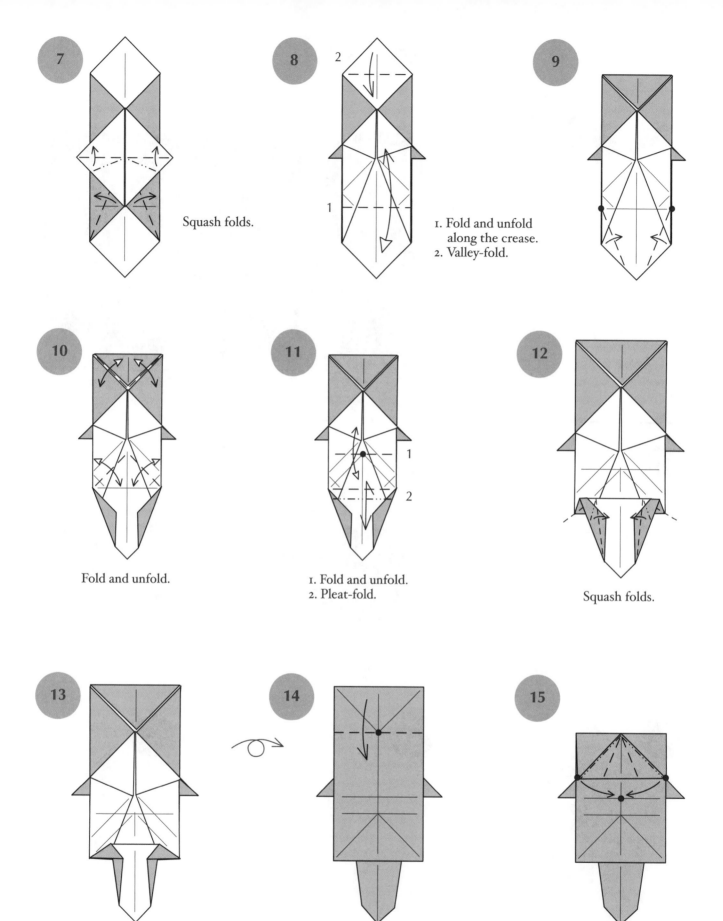

**7** Squash folds.

**8** 2 1
1. Fold and unfold along the crease.
2. Valley-fold.

**9**

**10** Fold and unfold.

**11** 1 2
1. Fold and unfold.
2. Pleat-fold.

**12** Squash folds.

**13**

**14**

**15** Squash folds.

**16**

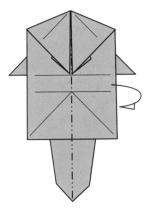

Fold in half and rotate.

**17**

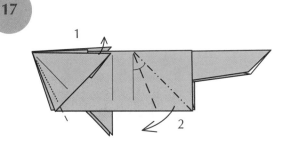

1. Slide the head up.
2. Crimp-fold.

**18**

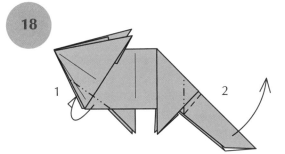

1. Fold inside, repeat behind.
2. Crimp-fold.

**19**

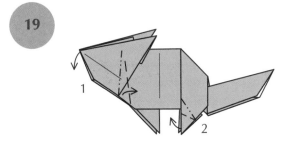

1. Crimp-fold.
2. Crimp-fold, repeat behind.

**20**

1. Squash-fold.
2. Valley-fold.
Repeat behind.

**21**

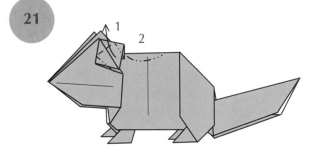

1. Petal-fold, repeat behind.
2. Shape the back.

**22**

**Chinchilla**

# Mouse

The domestic Mouse has been a pet for centuries. These small creatures can be easily trianed to sit on your hand, or climb your arm and sit on your shoulder. Though not as many Mice are kept as pets, they are quite popular and are quite intelligent.

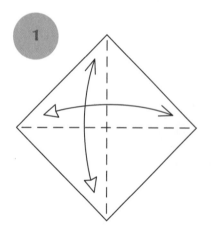

Fold and unfold.

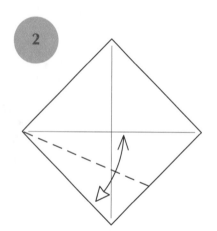

Fold and unfold.

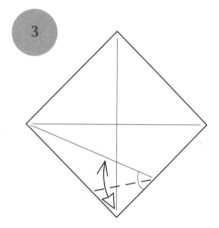

Fold and unfold.

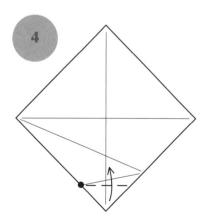

Fold and unfold.

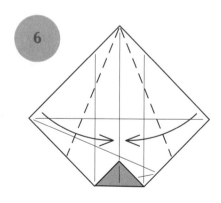

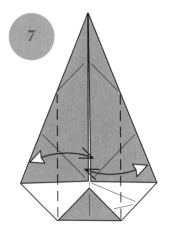

**7**

Fold and unfold along partially hidden creases.

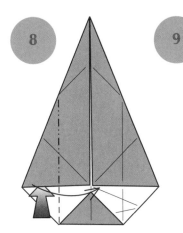

**8**

Reverse-fold.

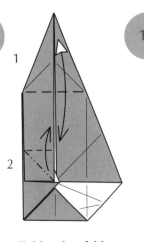

**9**

1. Fold and unfold.
2. Squash-fold.

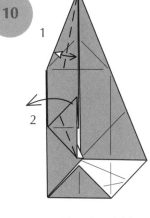

**10**

1. Fold and unfold.
2. Squash-fold.

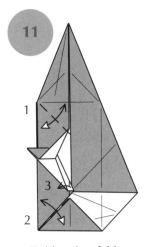

**11**

1. Fold and unfold.
2. Fold and unfold.
3. Valley-fold.

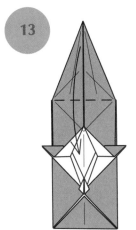

**12**

Repeat steps 8–11 on the right.

**13**

**14**

Fold and unfold.

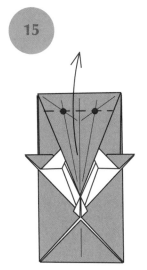

**15**

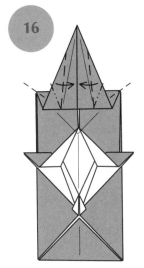

**16**

Squash folds. Do not fold to a point.

**17**

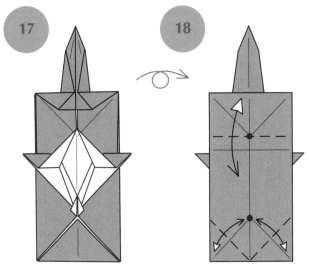

**18**

Fold and unfold.

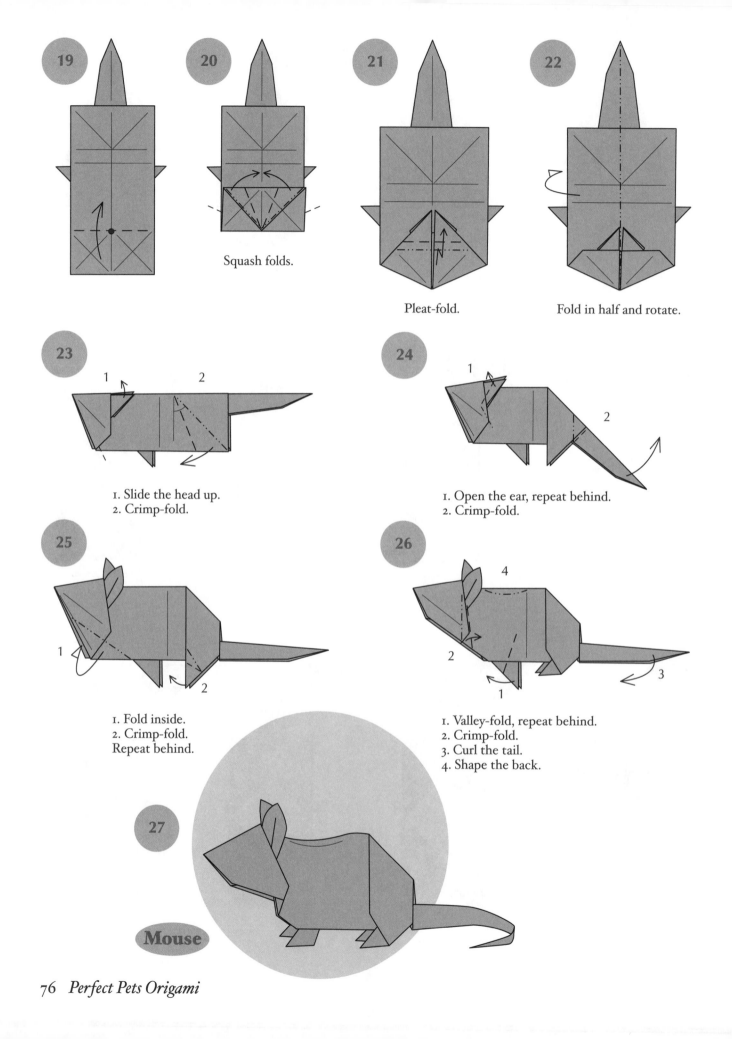

**19**

**20**

Squash folds.

**21**

Pleat-fold.

**22**

Fold in half and rotate.

**23**

1. Slide the head up.
2. Crimp-fold.

**24**

1. Open the ear, repeat behind.
2. Crimp-fold.

**25**

1. Fold inside.
2. Crimp-fold.
Repeat behind.

**26**

1. Valley-fold, repeat behind.
2. Crimp-fold.
3. Curl the tail.
4. Shape the back.

**27**

**Mouse**

# Ferret

The Ferret is a long, furry animal that resembles a weasel. Very popular as pets, there are even magazines for Ferret owners. Ferrets are believed to have been kept as domesticated pets for over two thousand years.

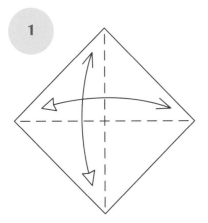

**1**

Fold and unfold.

**2**

Fold and unfold.

**3**

Fold and unfold on the diagonal.

**4**

**5**

Unfold.

**6**

Kite-fold.

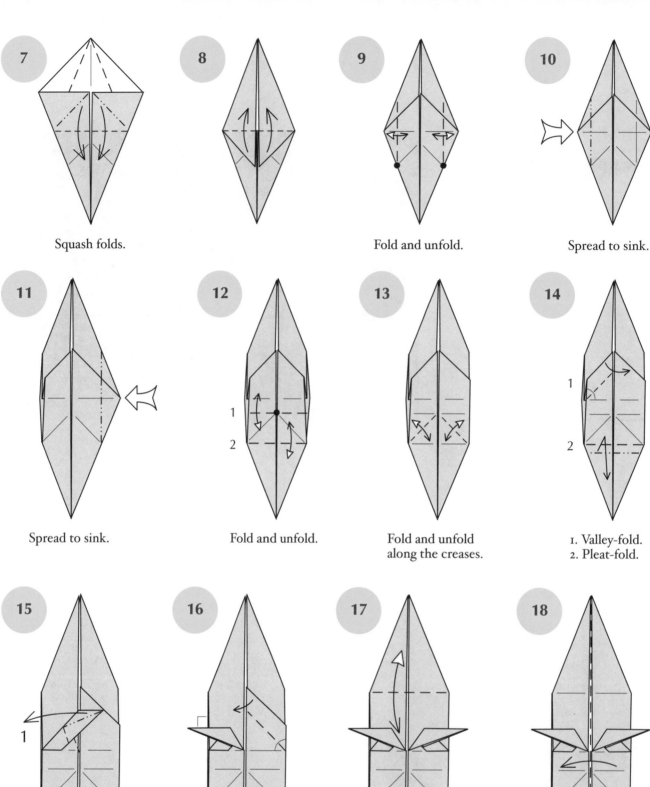

**7**

Squash folds.

**8**

**9**

Fold and unfold.

**10**

Spread to sink.

**11**

Spread to sink.

**12**

Fold and unfold.

**13**

Fold and unfold
along the creases.

**14**

1. Valley-fold.
2. Pleat-fold.

**15**

1. Squash-fold.
2. Squash folds.

**16**

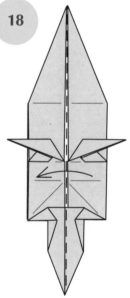

Note the right angle.
Repeat steps 14–15 on
the right for the leg.

**17**

Fold and unfold.

**18**

Fold in half
and rotate.

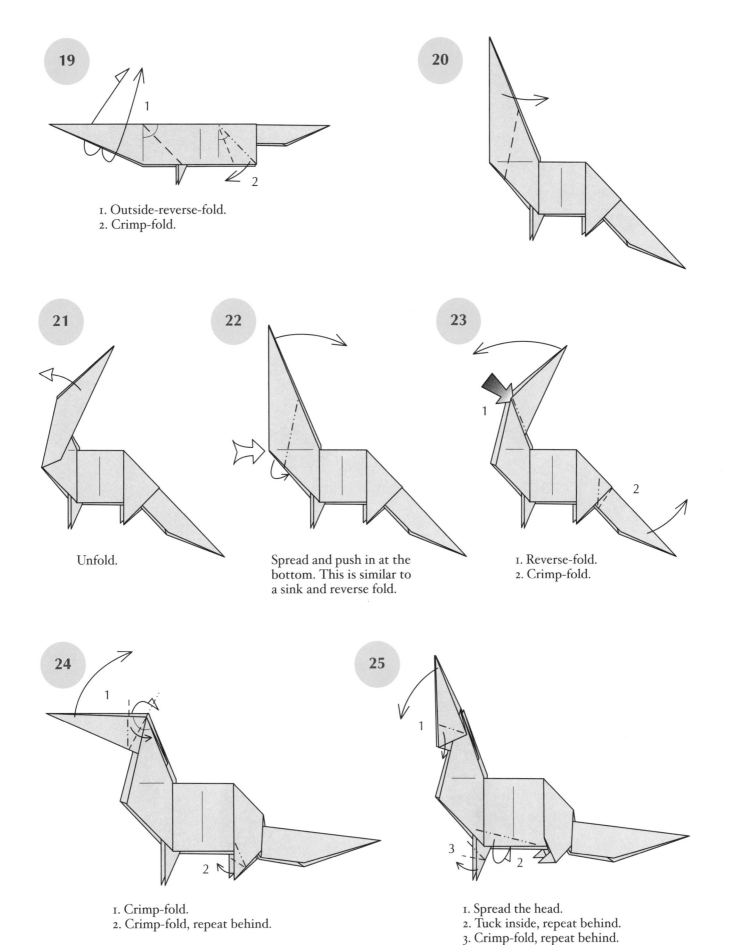

**19**

1. Outside-reverse-fold.
2. Crimp-fold.

**20**

**21**

Unfold.

**22**

Spread and push in at the bottom. This is similar to a sink and reverse fold.

**23**

1. Reverse-fold.
2. Crimp-fold.

**24**

1. Crimp-fold.
2. Crimp-fold, repeat behind.

**25**

1. Spread the head.
2. Tuck inside, repeat behind.
3. Crimp-fold, repeat behind.

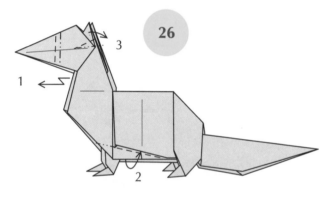

**26**

1. Crimp-fold.
2. Tuck inside, repeat behind.
3. Make a small squash fold,
   repeat behind.

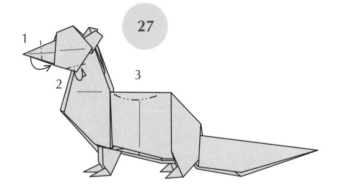

**27**

1. Reverse-fold.
2. Repeat behind.
3. Shape the back.

**28**

**Ferret**

# Gerbil

Like the Hamster and Mouse, the Gerbil is a small animal in the rodent family, and has also gone by the name "Desert Rat". Intelligent and cute, Gerbils are also very popular as pets for children and families.

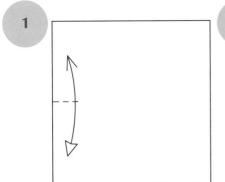

**1**

Fold and unfold on the left.

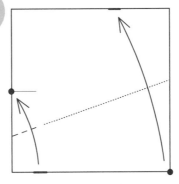

**2**

Bring the bottom right corner to the top and the bottom edge to the dot. Crease on the left.

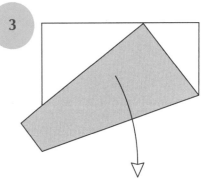

**3**

Unfold and rotate.

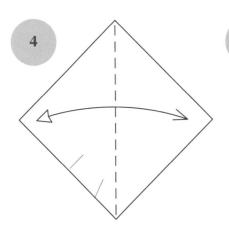

**4**

Fold and unfold.

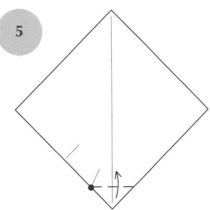

**5**

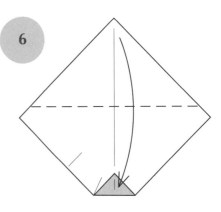

**6**

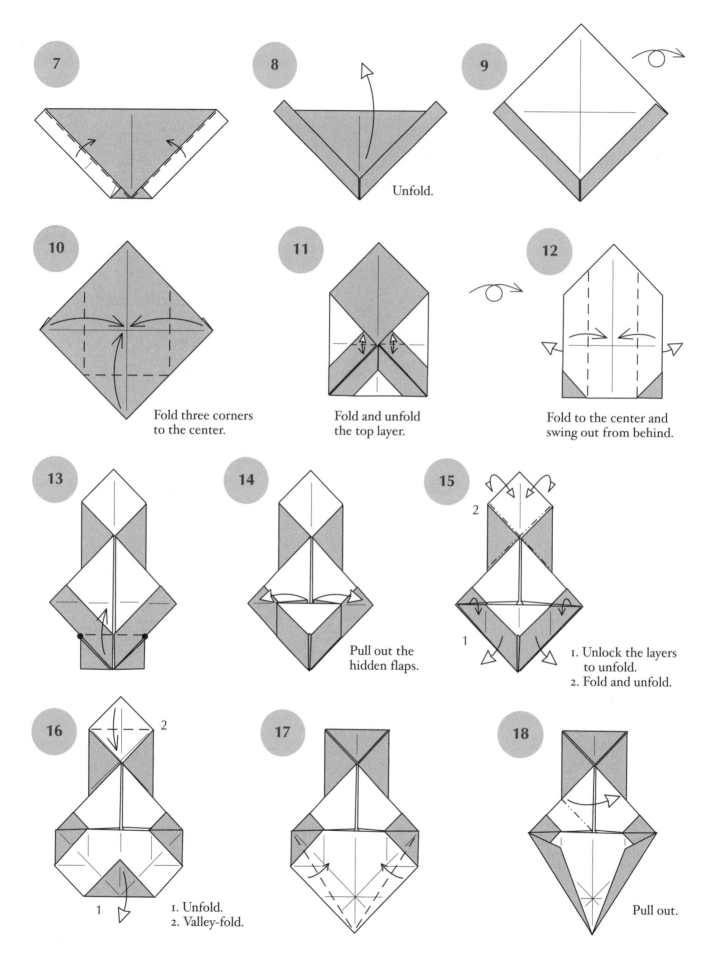

**7**

**8**

Unfold.

**9**

**10**

Fold three corners
to the center.

**11**

Fold and unfold
the top layer.

**12**

Fold to the center and
swing out from behind.

**13**

**14**

Pull out the
hidden flaps.

**15**

2

1

1. Unlock the layers
to unfold.
2. Fold and unfold.

**16**

2

1

1. Unfold.
2. Valley-fold.

**17**

**18**

Pull out.

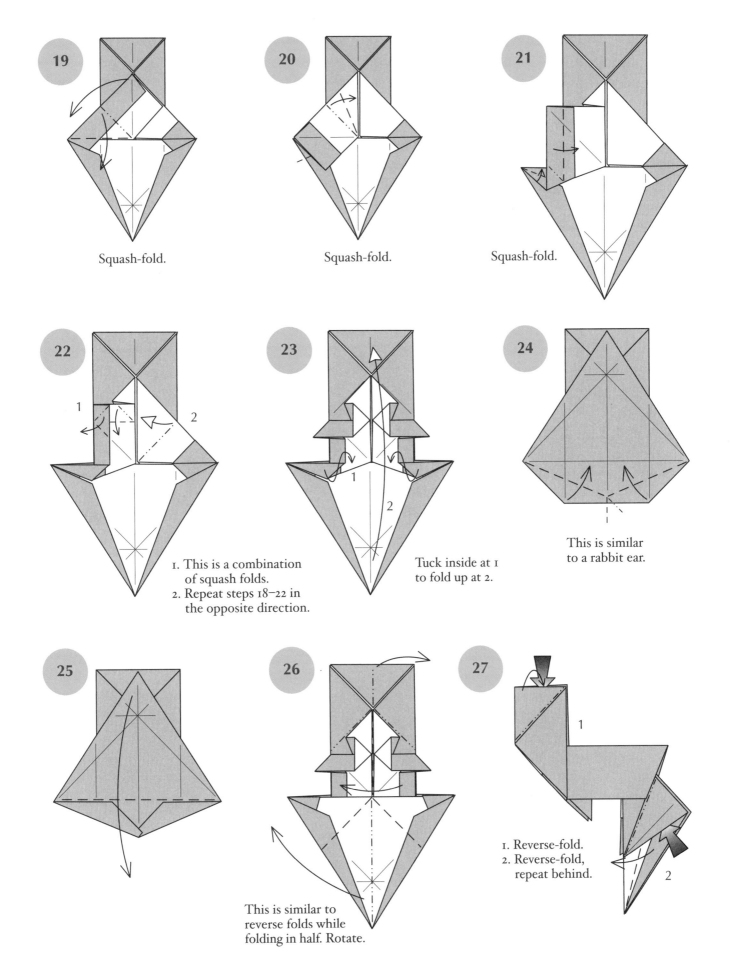

**19** Squash-fold.

**20** Squash-fold.

**21** Squash-fold.

**22**
1. This is a combination of squash folds.
2. Repeat steps 18–22 in the opposite direction.

**23** Tuck inside at 1 to fold up at 2.

**24** This is similar to a rabbit ear.

**25**

**26** This is similar to reverse folds while folding in half. Rotate.

**27**
1. Reverse-fold.
2. Reverse-fold, repeat behind.

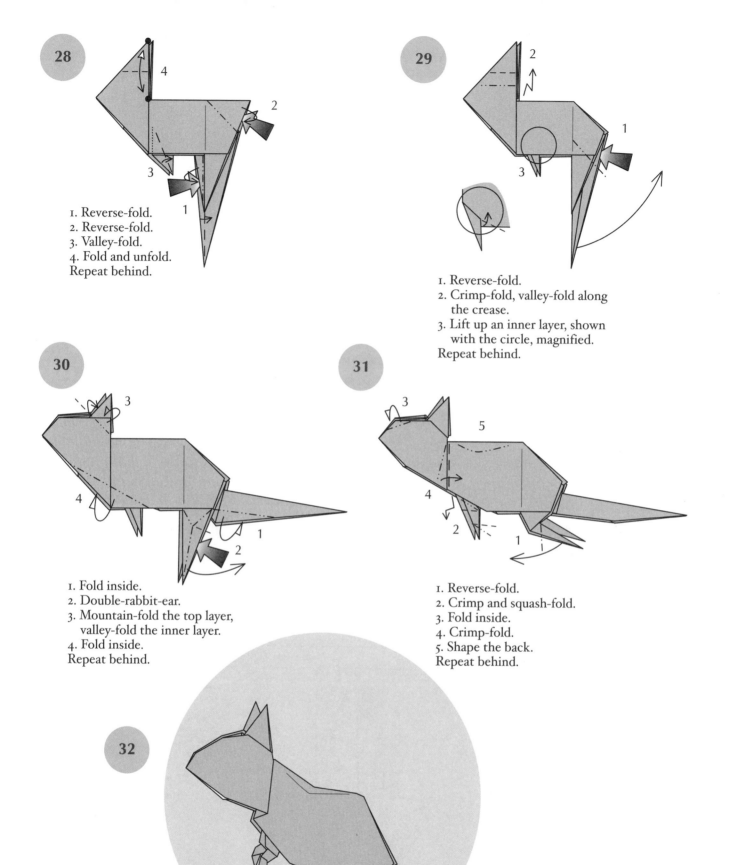

**28**

1. Reverse-fold.
2. Reverse-fold.
3. Valley-fold.
4. Fold and unfold.
Repeat behind.

**29**

1. Reverse-fold.
2. Crimp-fold, valley-fold along
   the crease.
3. Lift up an inner layer, shown
   with the circle, magnified.
Repeat behind.

**30**

1. Fold inside.
2. Double-rabbit-ear.
3. Mountain-fold the top layer,
   valley-fold the inner layer.
4. Fold inside.
Repeat behind.

**31**

1. Reverse-fold.
2. Crimp and squash-fold.
3. Fold inside.
4. Crimp-fold.
5. Shape the back.
Repeat behind.

**32**

**Gerbil**

# Rabbit

Rabbits are ideal pets for many people. These cute, fuzzy pets have distinct personalities, from very playful to shy. They are quiet, clean, and do not need much space. Rabbits are affectionate and bond with their owners. They enjoy toys and exploring their surroundings in a house. Rabbits can be trained to fetch, jump through hoops, and come to you on command.

**1**

Fold and unfold.

**2**

Bring the corner to the line.
Crease on the bottom half.

**3**

Unfold.

**4**

Repeat steps 2–3 in the
opposite direction.

**5**

Fold to the center.

**6**

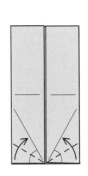

**7**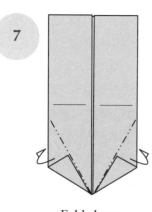

Fold along
the creases.

**8**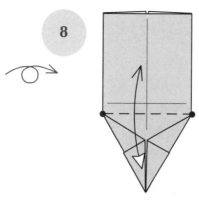

Fold and unfold.

**9**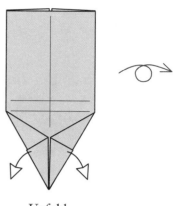

Unfold.

**10**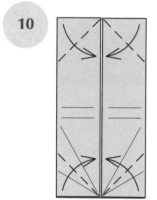

Fold to the center.

**11**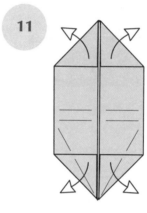

Unfold.

**12**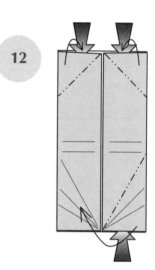

Fold along the creases
for these reverse folds.

**13**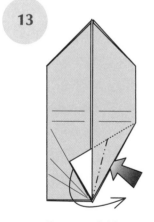

Reverse-fold
along the crease.

**14**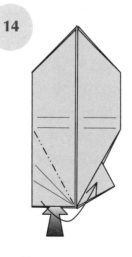

Repeat steps 12–13
on the bottom.

**15**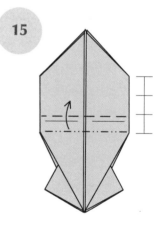

Pleat-fold. Mountain-fold
along the crease. Valley-fold
above the upper crease but
slightly below the 1/3 level.

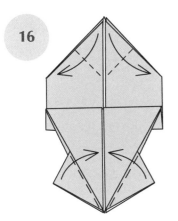

**16**

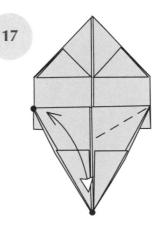

**17**

Fold and unfold.

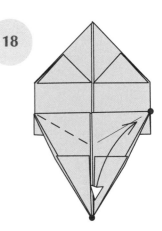

**18**

Fold and unfold.

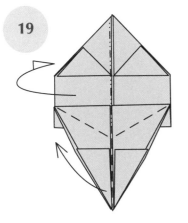

**19**

Fold the head up while folding the body in half. Rotate.

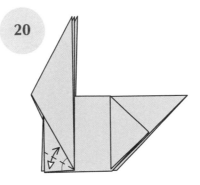

**20**

Fold and unfold along the crease. Repeat behind.

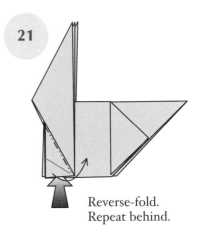

**21**

Reverse-fold. Repeat behind.

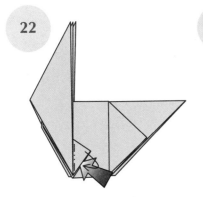

**22**

Reverse-fold. Repeat behind.

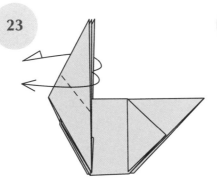

**23**

Outside-reverse-fold.

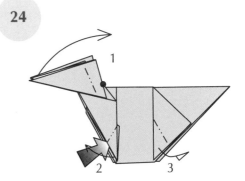

**24**

1. Reverse-fold so the ear meets the dot.
2. Reverse-fold.
3. Mountain-fold.
Repeat behind.

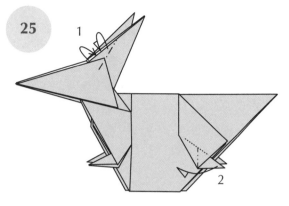

**25**

1. Fold inside on both sides of the ear.
2. Mountain-fold. Repeat behind.

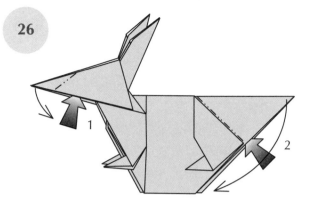

**26**

1. Reverse-fold.
2. Reverse-fold.

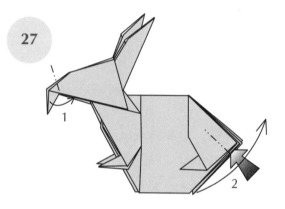

**27**

1. Reverse-fold several layers.
2. Reverse-fold the tail.

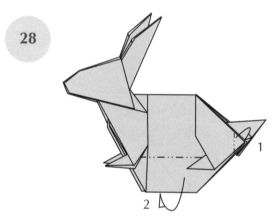

**28**

1. Mountain-fold one layer.
2. Fold inside. Repeat behind.

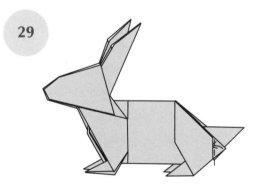

**29**

Valley-fold and repeat behind.

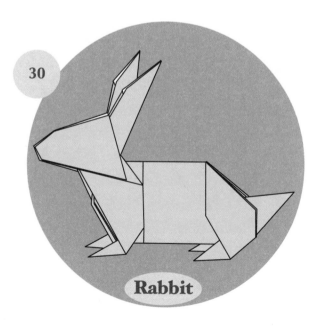

**30**

**Rabbit**

# Sitting Cat

Statues of Sitting Cats have been popular throughout the ages, and the Cats themselves have always seemed to have an aura of mystery about them due to their independent nature.

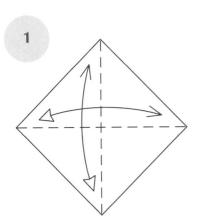

**1**

Fold and unfold.

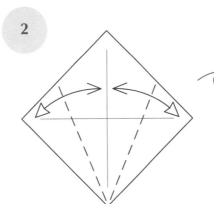

**2**

Kite-fold and unfold.

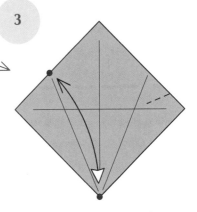

**3**

Fold and unfold on the edge. Rotate 180°.

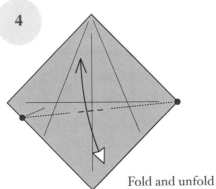

**4**

Fold and unfold along the diagonal.

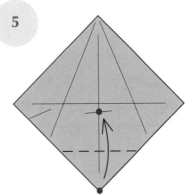

**5**

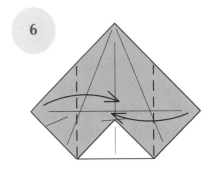

**6**

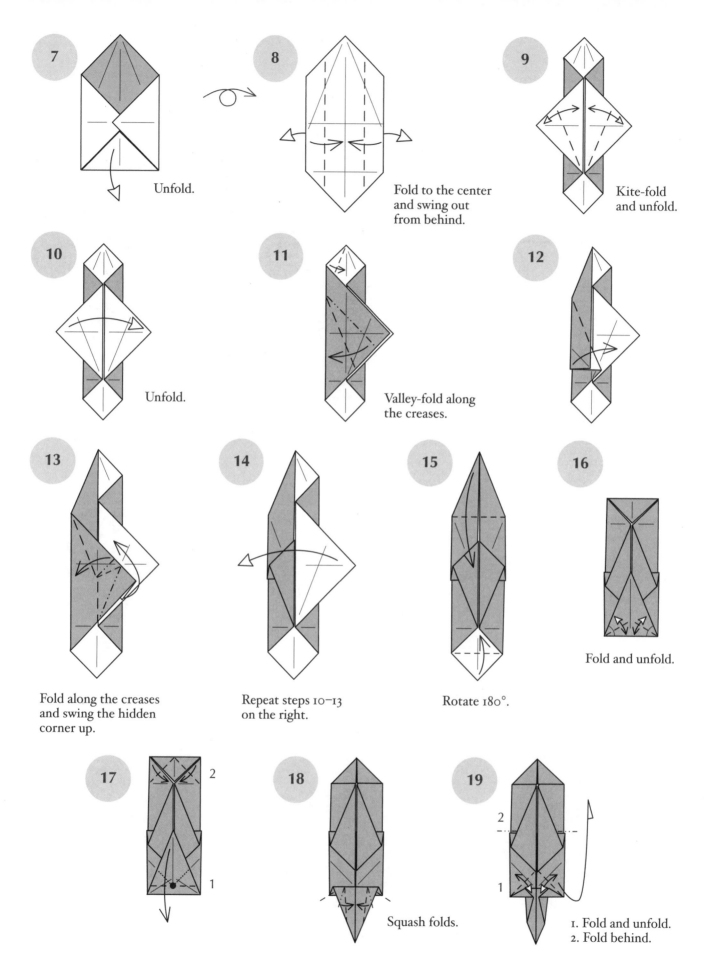

**7** Unfold.

**8** Fold to the center and swing out from behind.

**9** Kite-fold and unfold.

**10** Unfold.

**11** Valley-fold along the creases.

**12**

**13** Fold along the creases and swing the hidden corner up.

**14** Repeat steps 10–13 on the right.

**15** Rotate 180°.

**16** Fold and unfold.

**17**

**18** Squash folds.

**19** 1. Fold and unfold.
2. Fold behind.

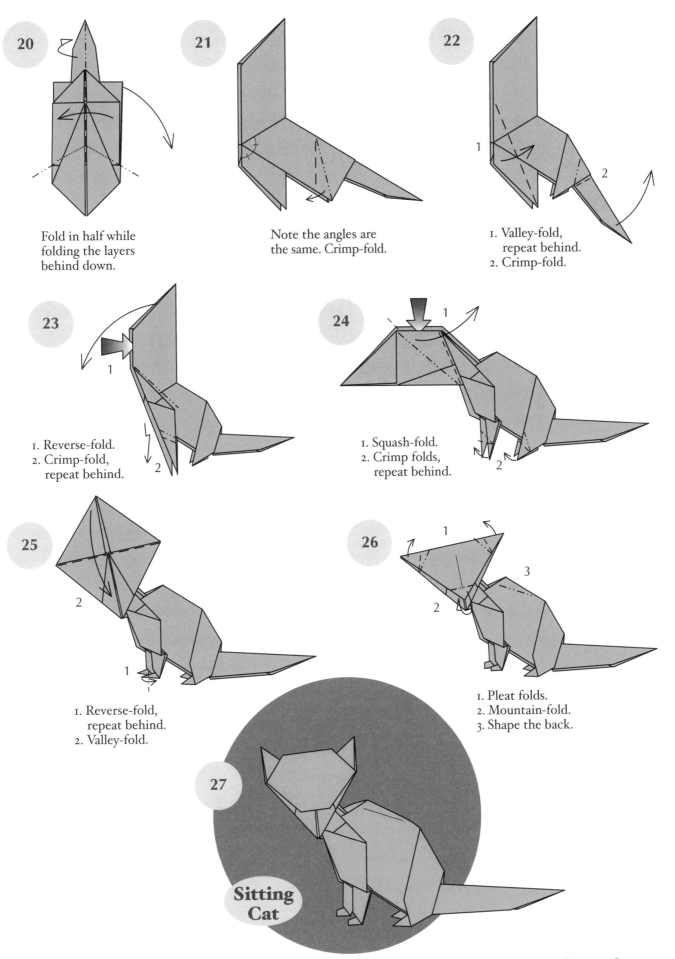

**20** Fold in half while folding the layers behind down.

**21** Note the angles are the same. Crimp-fold.

**22**
1. Valley-fold, repeat behind.
2. Crimp-fold.

**23**
1. Reverse-fold.
2. Crimp-fold, repeat behind.

**24**
1. Squash-fold.
2. Crimp folds, repeat behind.

**25**
1. Reverse-fold, repeat behind.
2. Valley-fold.

**26**
1. Pleat folds.
2. Mountain-fold.
3. Shape the back.

**27**

**Sitting Cat**

# Standing Cat

The Cat was once revered in ancient Egypt as being divine, and has held a special place in popular culture for thousands of years. Cats are often said to have nine lives due to their ability to survive what seem to be insurmountable dangers. They enjoy being near its owners but does not require constant attention.

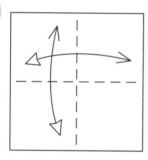

**1**

Fold and unfold.

**2**

Bring the corner to the line.
Crease on the bottom half.

**3**

Unfold.

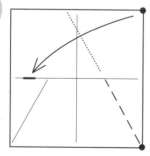

**4**

Repeat steps 2–3 in the opposite direction.

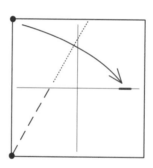

**5**

Fold to the center.

**6**

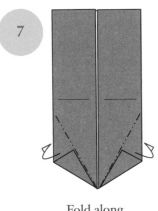

**7** Fold along the creases.

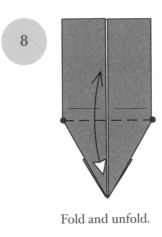
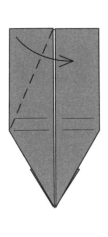

**8** Fold and unfold.

**9**

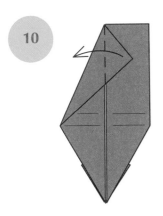

**10**

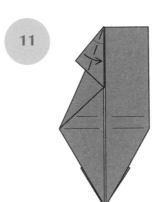

**11**

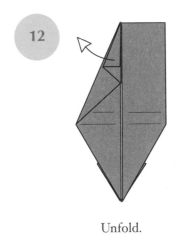

**12** Unfold.

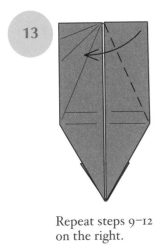

**13** Repeat steps 9–12 on the right.

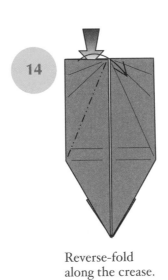

**14** Reverse-fold along the crease.

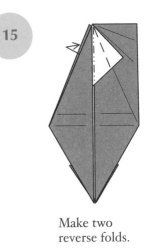

**15** Make two reverse folds.

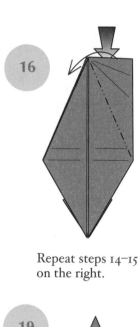

**16**

Repeat steps 14–15 on the right.

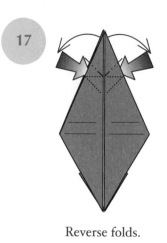

**17**

Reverse folds.

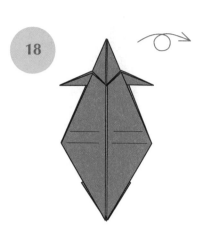

**18**

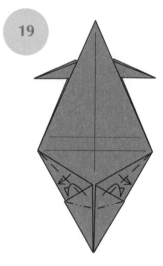

**19**

This is similar to reverse folds.

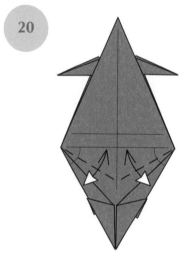

**20**

Fold and unfold.

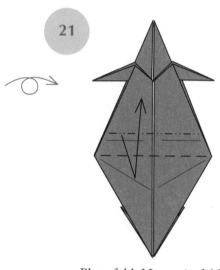

**21**

Pleat-fold. Mountain-fold slightly above the creases.

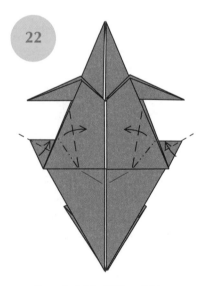

**22**

Squash folds. Valley-fold on the left and right along partially hidden creases.

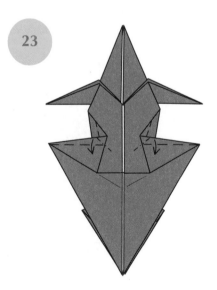

**23**

Squash folds.

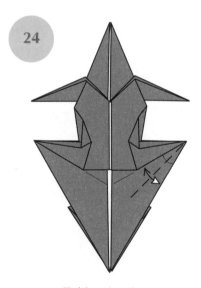

**24**

Fold and unfold.

**25**

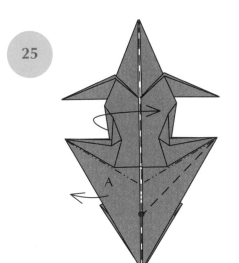

Fold the body in half while bringing the head up. Push in at the dot. Region A will show in the next step. Rotate.

**26**

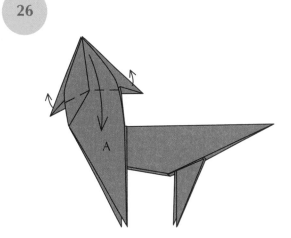

This is 3D. Flatten.

**27**

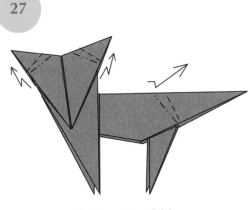

Make crimp folds.

**28**

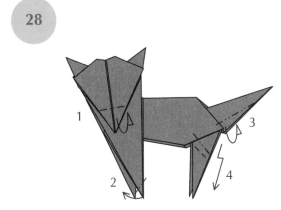

1. Mountain-fold.
2. Reverse-fold, repeat behind.
3. Fold inside, repeat behind.
4. Crimp-fold, repeat behind.

**29**

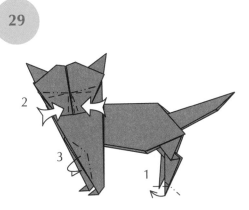

1. Crimp-fold, repeat behind.
2. Shape the face with soft folds.
3. Shape the legs, repeat behind.

**30**

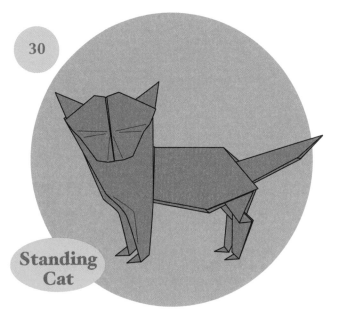

Standing Cat

# Walking Cat

Sometimes cats seem very standoffish or almost regal as they walk, which fits with their independent personalities. Even when you gain the trust of cats, they still sometimes prefer to be alone or not be bothered if they are around humans. But for all those traits, a cat will let you know it likes and trusts you, and will often show it by walking up to you and leaning on you.

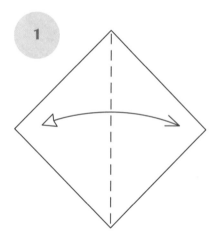

Fold and unfold.

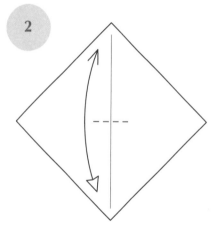

Fold and unfold in the center.

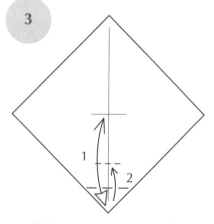

1. Fold to the center and unfold.
2. Fold up to the crease.

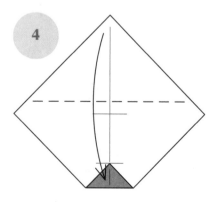

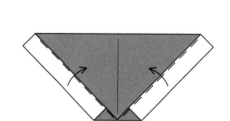

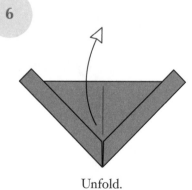

Unfold.

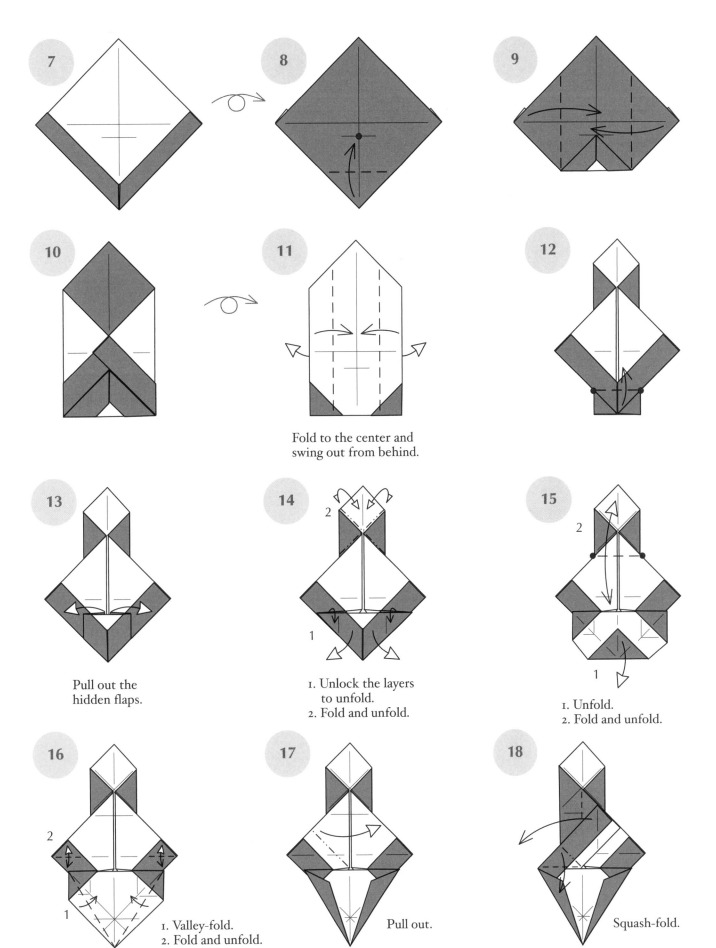

**11**

Fold to the center and
swing out from behind.

**13**

Pull out the
hidden flaps.

**14**

1. Unlock the layers
   to unfold.
2. Fold and unfold.

**15**

1. Unfold.
2. Fold and unfold.

**16**

1. Valley-fold.
2. Fold and unfold.

**17**

Pull out.

**18**

Squash-fold.

*Walking Cat* 97

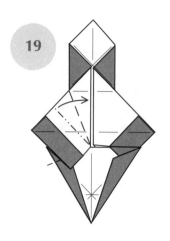

**19**

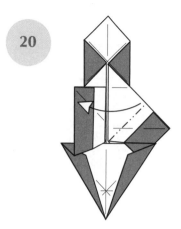

**20**

Repeat steps 17–19 in
the opposite direction.

**21**

2

1

1. Fold and unfold.
2. Valley-fold.

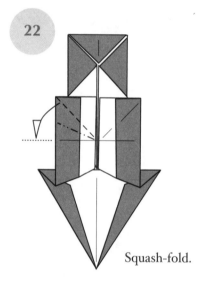

**22**

Squash-fold.

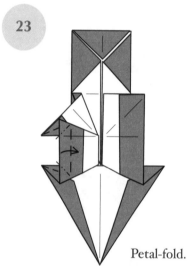

**23**

Petal-fold.

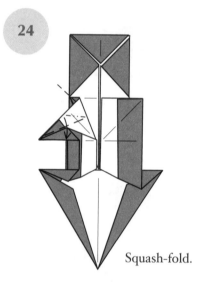

**24**

Squash-fold.

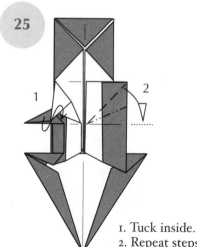

**25**

1

2

1. Tuck inside.
2. Repeat steps 22–25
   on the right.

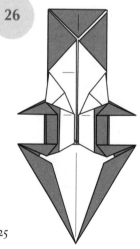

**26**

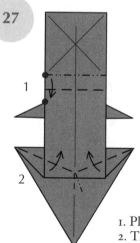

**27**

1

2

1. Pleat-fold.
2. This is similar
   to a rabbit ear.

**28**

This is similar to reverse folds while folding in half. Rotate.

**29**

1. Reverse-fold, repeat behind.
2. Reverse-fold.
3. Fold inside, repeat behind.

**30**

1. Reverse-fold, repeat behind.
2. Reverse-fold.
3. Crimp-fold, repeat behind.

**31**

1. Crimp-fold.
2. Fold inside, repeat behind.

**32**

1. Reverse-fold.
2. Crimp-fold, repeat behind.
3. Pleat-fold, repeat behind.

**33**

1. Crimp-fold and spread the tail.
2. Shape the foot, repeat behind.
3. Reverse-fold, repeat behind.
4. Make a small crimp fold to shape the body.

**34**

**Walking Cat**

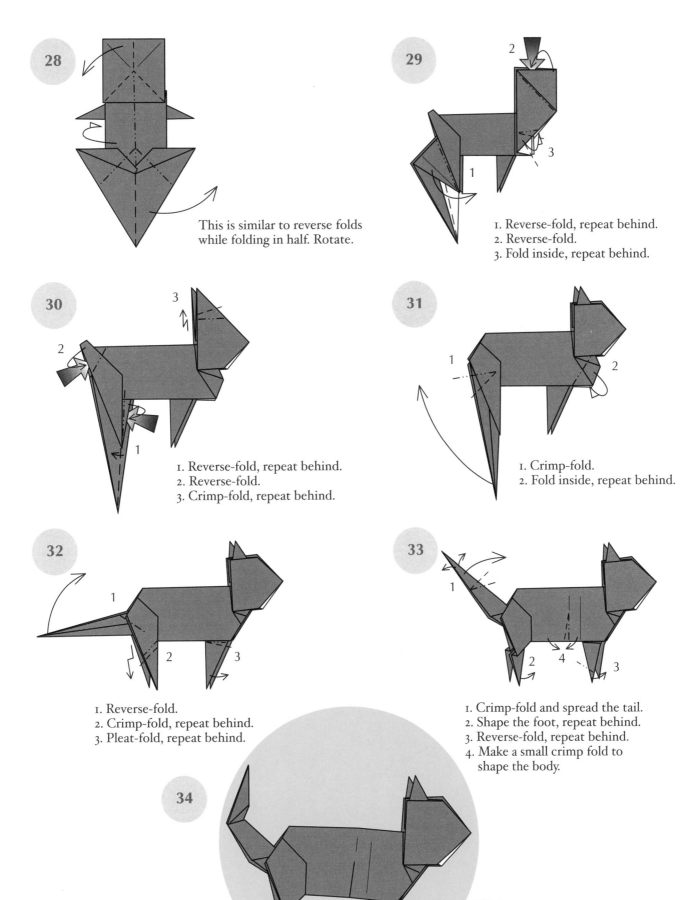

# Beagle

The Beagle is a smaller dog with big floppy ears and has held a place in popular culture for hundreds of years. With its keen sense of smell, the beagle has been used for centuries as a scent hound in hunting and even in law enforcement. Beagles are affectionate and playful with children.

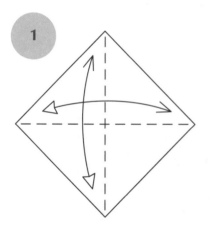

Fold and unfold.

Kite-fold and unfold.

Bring the corners to the dots.

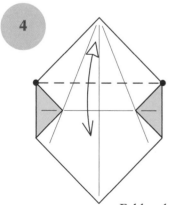

Fold and unfold.

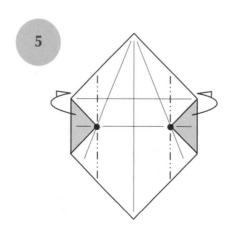

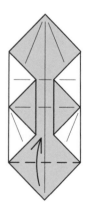

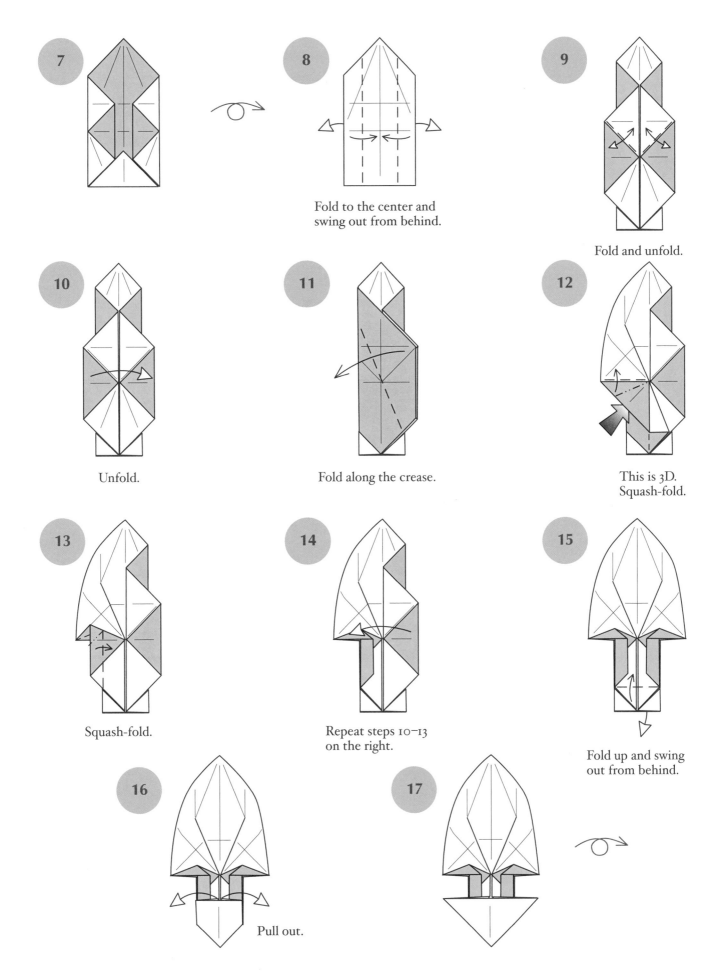

**7**

**8**

Fold to the center and
swing out from behind.

**9**

Fold and unfold.

**10**

Unfold.

**11**

Fold along the crease.

**12**

This is 3D.
Squash-fold.

**13**

Squash-fold.

**14**

Repeat steps 10–13
on the right.

**15**

Fold up and swing
out from behind.

**16**

Pull out.

**17**

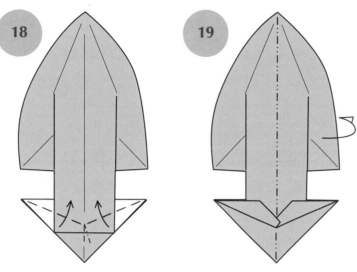

**18**

**19**

Fold in half and rotate 90°.

**20**

This is still 3D. Fold along the creases on both sides. This is similar to a double rabbit ear.

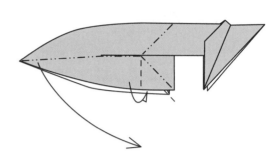

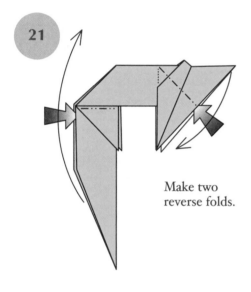

**21**

Make two reverse folds.

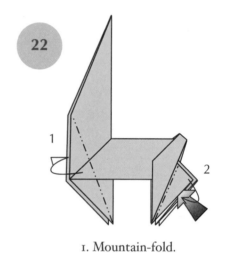

**22**

1. Mountain-fold.
2. Reverse-fold.
Repeat behind.

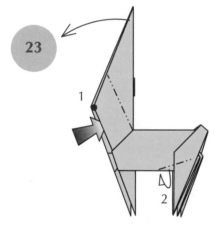

**23**

1. Reverse-fold so the bold line meets the dot.
2. Mountain-fold, repeat behind.

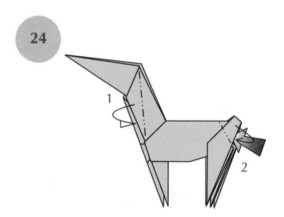

**24**

1. Mountain-fold, repeat behind.
2. Reverse-fold.

**25**

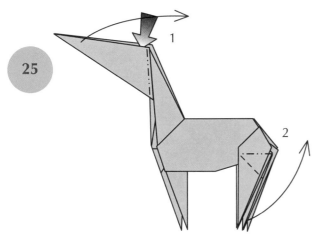

1. Reverse-fold.
2. Crimp-fold.

**26**

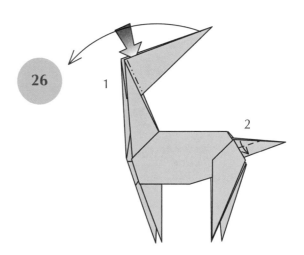

1. Reverse-fold.
2. Thin the tail with reverse folds, repeat behind.

**27**

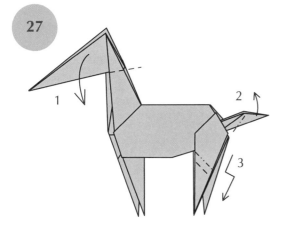

1. Fold down, repeat behind.
2. Reverse-fold.
3. Crimp-fold, repeat behind.

**28**

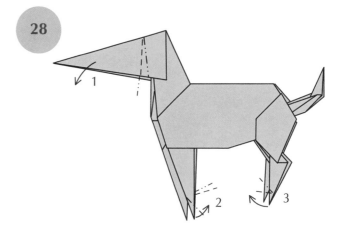

1. Crimp-fold.
2. Squash-fold.
3. Crimp-fold.
Repeat behind.

**29**

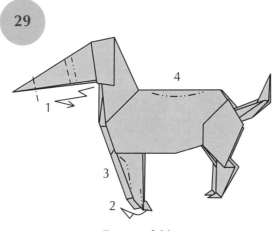

1. Reverse folds.
2. Mountain-fold.
3. Shape the legs.
4. Shape the back.
Repeat behind.

**30**

**Beagle**

# Collie

The Collie is a very intelligent dog that has been used throughout the centuries to herd other animals such as sheep. Collies have a lot of energy and are popular as both work and show dogs. Playful and gentle around childern, they also enjoy long walks. Collies are careful with other small family pets.

**1**

Fold in half.

**2**

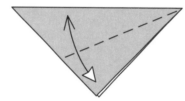

Fold and unfold the top layer. Repeat behind.

**3**

Fold and unfold.

**4**

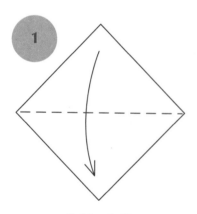

Reverse-fold.

**5**

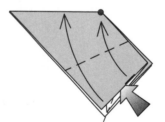

Squash-fold along the crease. Repeat behind.

**6**

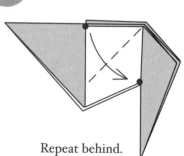

Repeat behind.

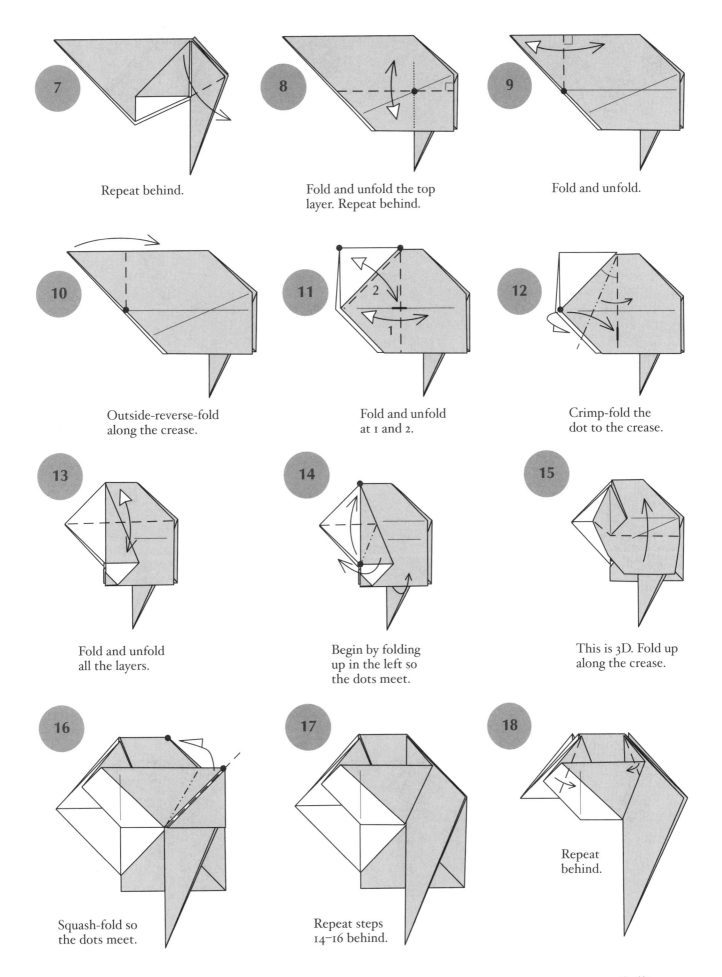

**7** Repeat behind.

**8** Fold and unfold the top layer. Repeat behind.

**9** Fold and unfold.

**10** Outside-reverse-fold along the crease.

**11** Fold and unfold at 1 and 2.

**12** Crimp-fold the dot to the crease.

**13** Fold and unfold all the layers.

**14** Begin by folding up in the left so the dots meet.

**15** This is 3D. Fold up along the crease.

**16** Squash-fold so the dots meet.

**17** Repeat steps 14–16 behind.

**18** Repeat behind.

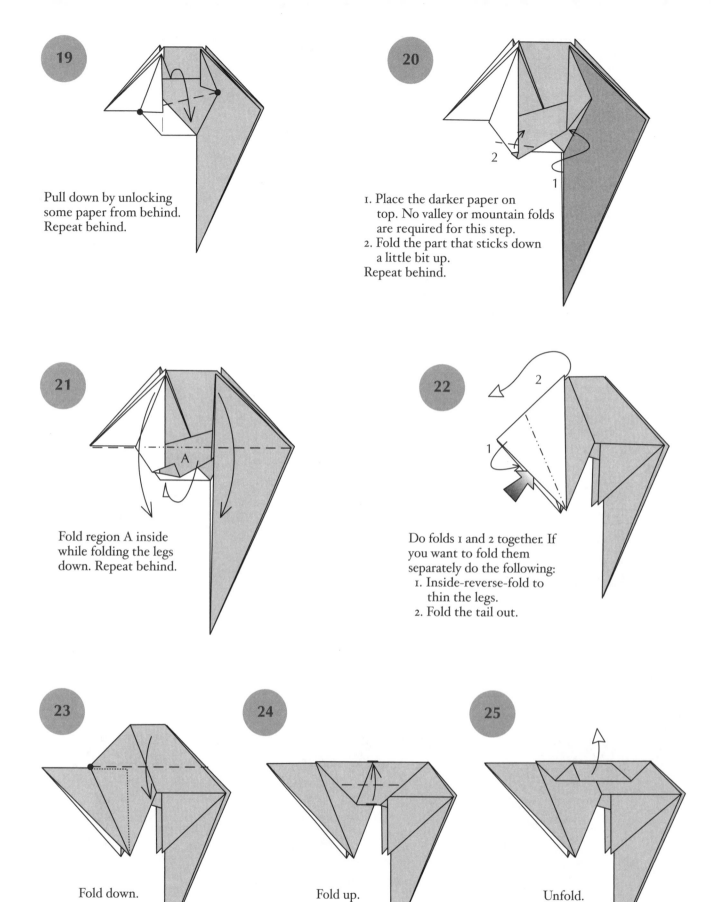

**19**

Pull down by unlocking
some paper from behind.
Repeat behind.

**20**

1. Place the darker paper on
   top. No valley or mountain folds
   are required for this step.
2. Fold the part that sticks down
   a little bit up.
Repeat behind.

**21**

Fold region A inside
while folding the legs
down. Repeat behind.

**22**

Do folds 1 and 2 together. If
you want to fold them
separately do the following:
  1. Inside-reverse-fold to
     thin the legs.
  2. Fold the tail out.

**23**

Fold down.

**24**

Fold up.

**25**

Unfold.

**26**

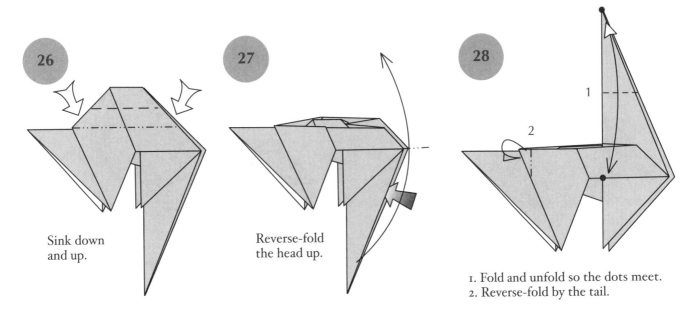

Sink down and up.

**27**

Reverse-fold the head up.

**28**

1. Fold and unfold so the dots meet.
2. Reverse-fold by the tail.

**29**

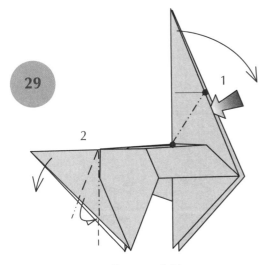

1. Reverse-fold.
2. Crimp-fold.

**30**

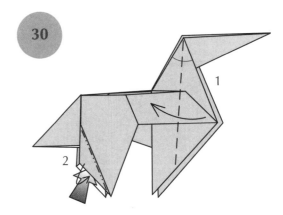

1. Bisect the angle.
2. Reverse-fold.
Repeat behind.

**31**

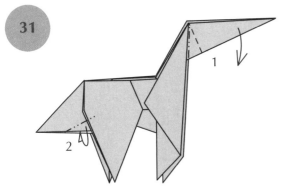

1. Valley-fold along the crease for this crimp fold.
2. Make a small, hidden squash fold and repeat behind.

**32**

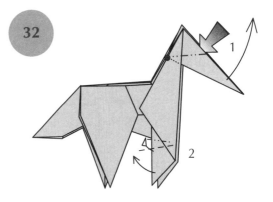

1. Reverse-fold.
2. Pleat-fold and repeat behind.

**33**

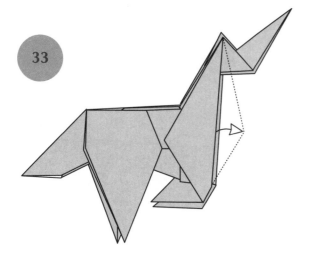

Pull out. Repeat behind.

**34**

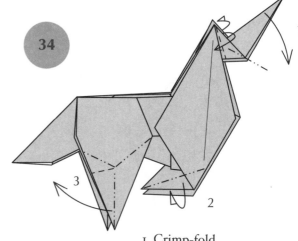

1. Crimp-fold.
2. Fold behind.
3. Rabbit-ear.
Repeat behind.

**35**

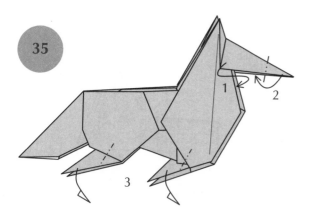

1. Tuck inside.
2. Reverse-fold.
3. Fold behind.
Repeat behind.

**36**

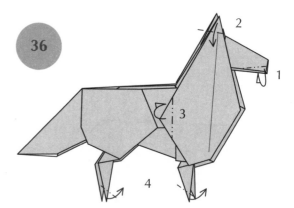

1. Fold inside.
2. Fold down.
3. Fold behind.
4. Reverse folds.
Repeat behind.

**37**

**Collie**

# Pot-Bellied Pig

Pot-Bellied Pigs can be very fun pets to raise inside the house. Often taken in as Piglets, most Pot-Bellied Pigs do grow up to be quite large, and contrary to expectations, they tend to be very clean animals. They are also very intelligent. Distinctive features of the Pot-Bellied Pigs include a long tuft of bristles along the backbone from head to tail as well as a very fleshy face, the eyes almost hidden in folds of skin.

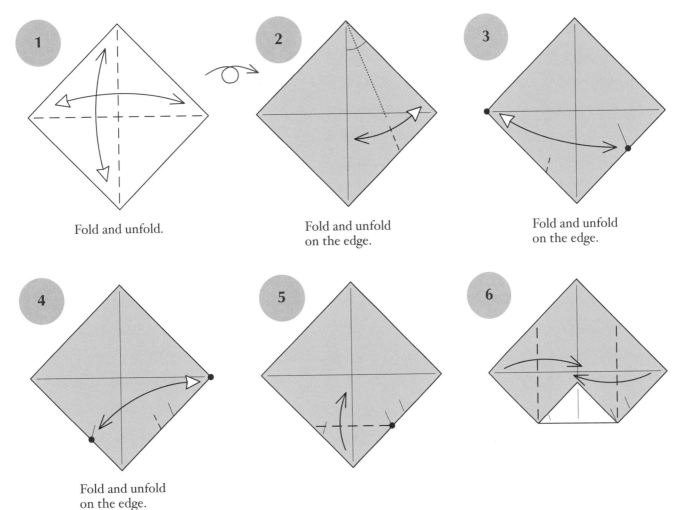

**1** Fold and unfold.

**2** Fold and unfold on the edge.

**3** Fold and unfold on the edge.

**4** Fold and unfold on the edge.

**5**

**6**

**7**

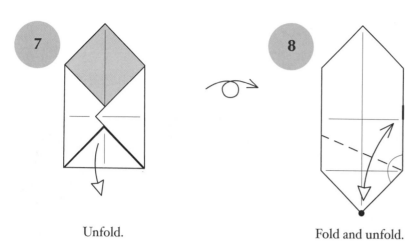

Unfold.

**8**

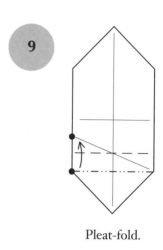

Fold and unfold.

**9**

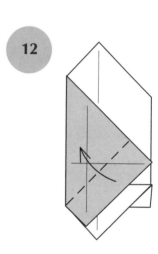

Pleat-fold.

**10**

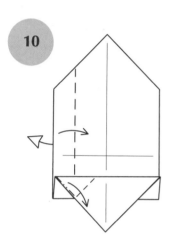

Squash-fold and swing
out from behind.

**11**

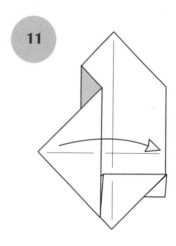

Unfold.

**12**

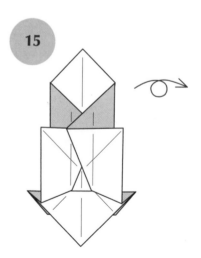

**13**

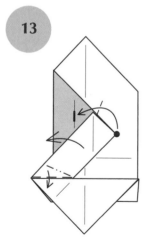

Squash-fold so the
dot meets the line.

**14**

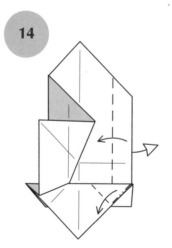

Repeat steps 10–13
on the right.

**15**

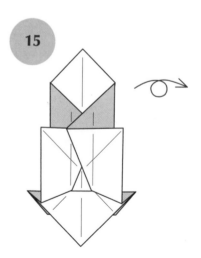

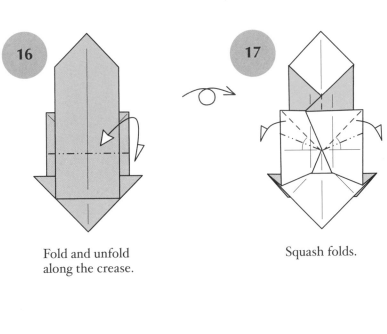

**16**

Fold and unfold along the crease.

**17**

Squash folds.

**18**

1. Valley-fold.
2. Petal-fold.

**19**

Wrap around.

**20**

1. Spread-squash-fold.
2. Fold and unfold.
3. Fold and unfold.

**21**

Repeat steps 18–20 on the right.

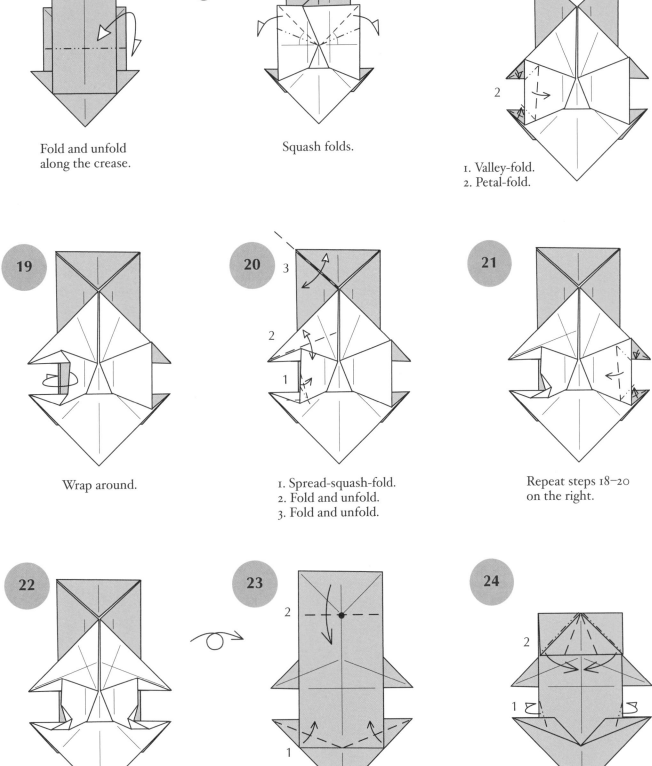

**22**

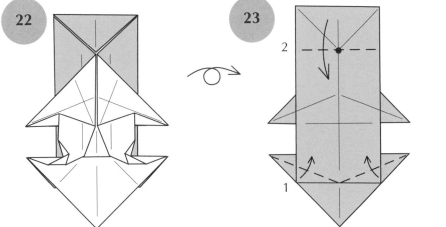

**23**

**24**

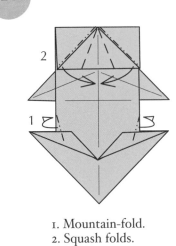

1. Mountain-fold.
2. Squash folds.

**25**

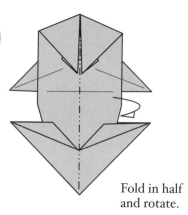

Fold in half
and rotate.

**26**

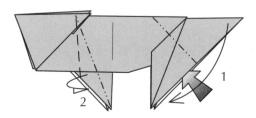

1. Reverse-fold.
2. Crimp-fold.

**27**

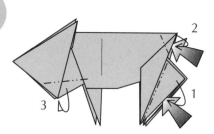

1. Reverse-fold, repeat behind.
2. Reverse-fold.
3. Fold inside, repeat behind.

**28**

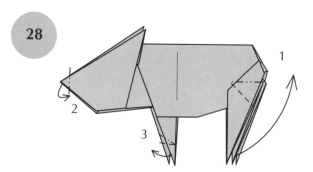

1. Crimp-fold.
2. Reverse-fold.
3. Crimp-fold, repeat behind.

**29**

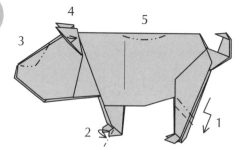

1. Valley-fold.
2. Reverse-fold.
3. Spread.
4. Reverse folds.
Repeat behind.

**30**

1. Crimp-fold.
2. Reverse-fold.
3. Shape the head and snout.
4. Open a bit.
5. Shape the back.
Repeat behind.

**31**

**Pot-Bellied Pig**

# Squirrel Monkey

Though more common as pets in the 1970's and before, Squirrel Monkeys are small, intelligent primates. Tougher laws and a decrease in the Squirrel Monkey population has led to their being less common as pets in the twenty-first century, but they love to eat bananas, climb trees, and are very curious.

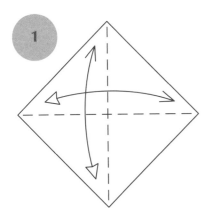

**1**

Fold and unfold.

**2**

Fold and unfold
on the edge.

**3**

Fold and unfold
on the edge.

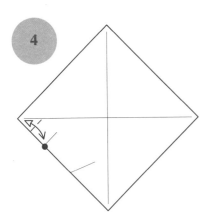

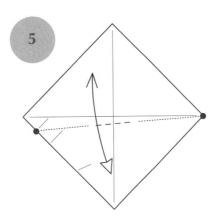

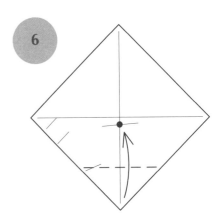

**4**

Fold and unfold
on the edge.

**5**

Fold and unfold
on the diagonal.

**6**

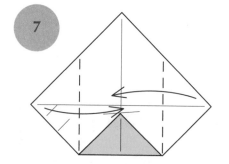

**7**

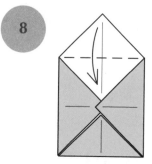

**8**

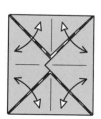

**9**

Fold and unfold.

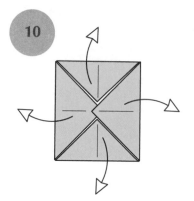

**10**

Unfold.

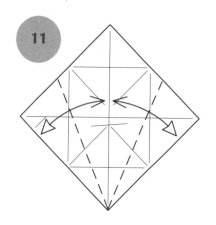

**11**

Kite-fold and unfold.

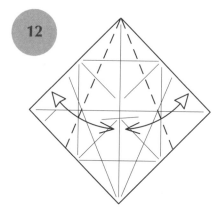

**12**

Kite-fold and unfold.

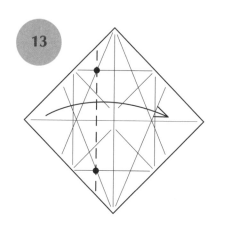

**13**

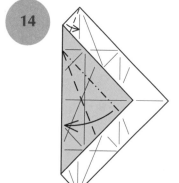

**14**

Valley-fold along
the creases.

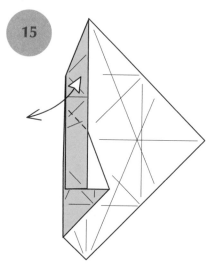

**15**

Fold and unfold along a
hidden crease. (Turn
over to see the crease.)

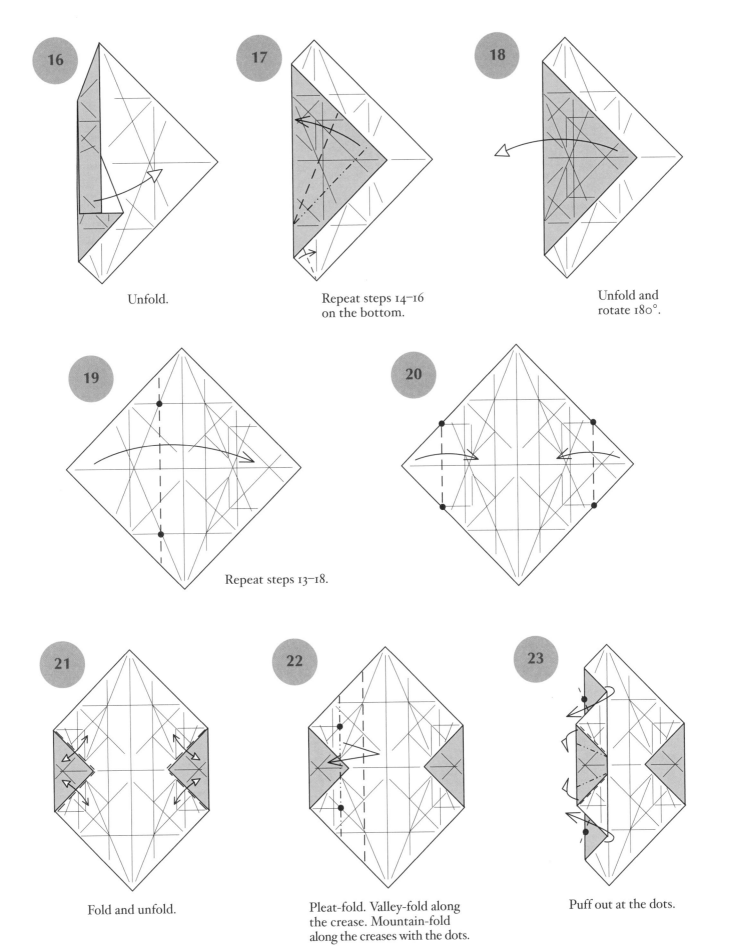

**16**

Unfold.

**17**

Repeat steps 14–16 on the bottom.

**18**

Unfold and rotate 180°.

**19**

Repeat steps 13–18.

**20**

**21**

Fold and unfold.

**22**

Pleat-fold. Valley-fold along the crease. Mountain-fold along the creases with the dots.

**23**

Puff out at the dots.

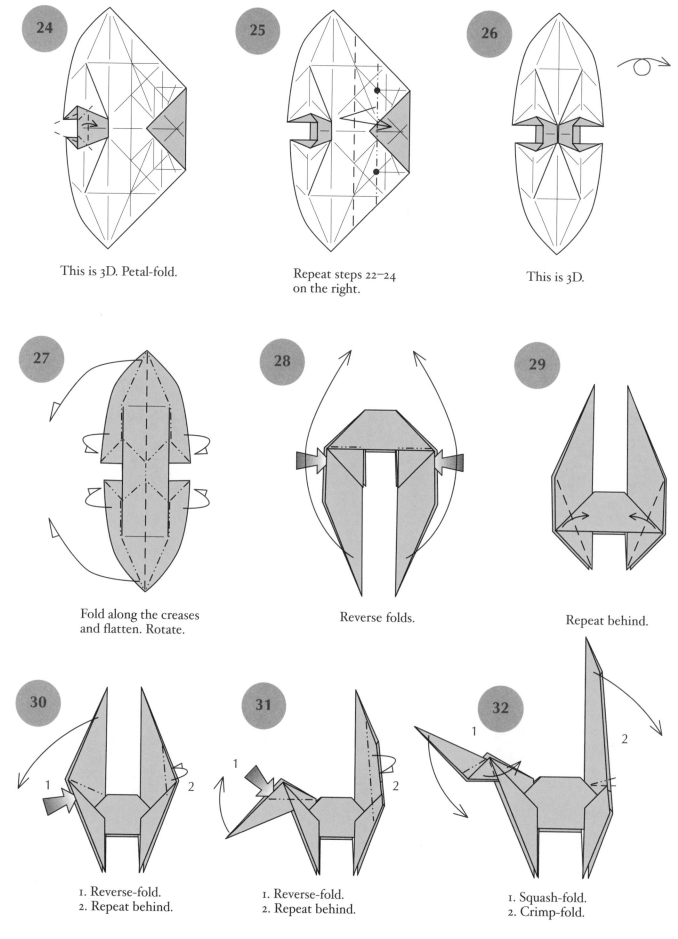

**24**

This is 3D. Petal-fold.

**25**

Repeat steps 22–24 on the right.

**26**

This is 3D.

**27**

Fold along the creases and flatten. Rotate.

**28**

Reverse folds.

**29**

Repeat behind.

**30**

1. Reverse-fold.
2. Repeat behind.

**31**

1. Reverse-fold.
2. Repeat behind.

**32**

1. Squash-fold.
2. Crimp-fold.

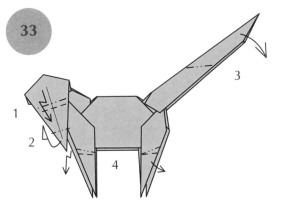

**33**

1. Pleat-fold.
2. Mountain-fold.
3. Reverse-fold.
4. Crimp folds, repeat behind.

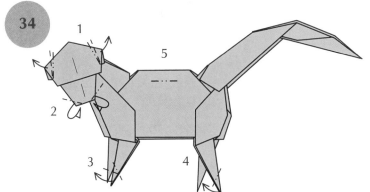

**34**

1. Pleat folds.
2. Mountain folds.
3. Crimp-fold, repeat behind.
4. Reverse-fold, repeat behind.
5. Shape the back.

**35**

**Squirrel Monkey**

# Bugs

Spiders, insects, and other arthropods make for interesting pets. Centipedes, millipedes, beetles, walking sticks, and even some cockroach varieties are some of the popular pets. In Japan, children enjoy keeping cicadas and beetles. Some of these little creatures are fun to hold as they walk across your hands. Often, these pets are released into the wild.

## Cicada

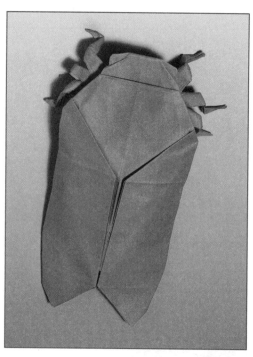

Cicadas are rather difficult to keep as pets due to their complex feeing needs, but some people are willing to put in the time and effort to keep them. Most Cicadas have a lifespan in captivity of 2 or 3 years, though the famous Periodical Cicada lives around 17 years.

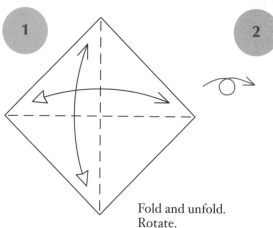

**1**

Fold and unfold.
Rotate.

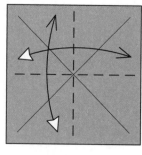

**2**

Fold and unfold.

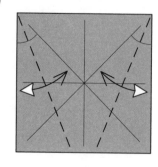

**3**

Fold and unfold.

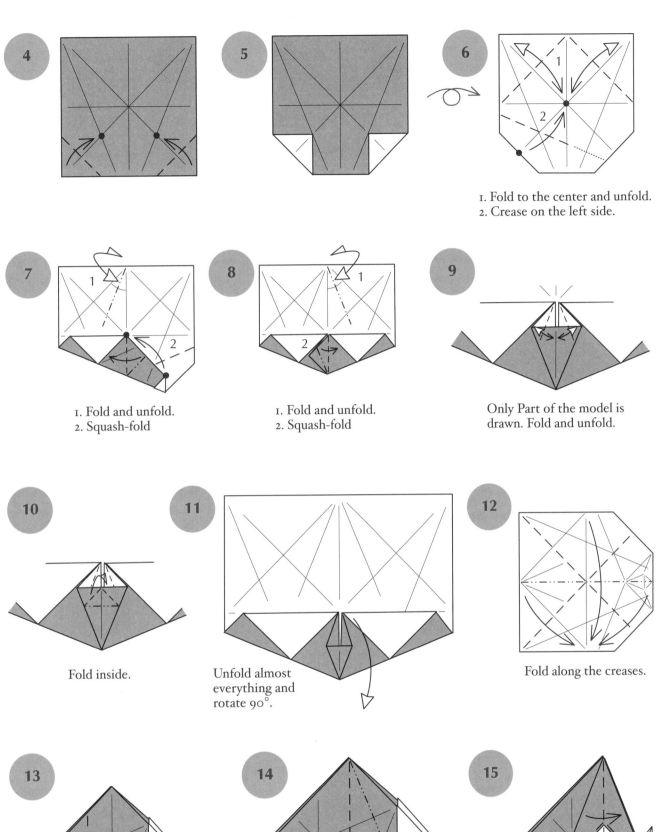

**4**

**5**

**6**

1. Fold to the center and unfold.
2. Crease on the left side.

**7**

1. Fold and unfold.
2. Squash-fold

**8**

1. Fold and unfold.
2. Squash-fold

**9**

Only Part of the model is drawn. Fold and unfold.

**10**

Fold inside.

**11**

Unfold almost everything and rotate 90°.

**12**

Fold along the creases.

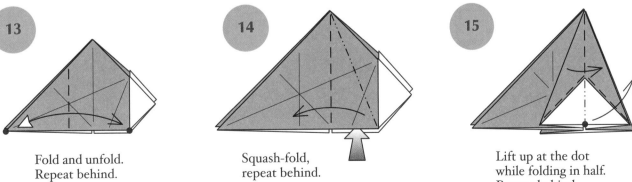

**13**

Fold and unfold. Repeat behind.

**14**

Squash-fold, repeat behind.

**15**

Lift up at the dot while folding in half. Repeat behind.

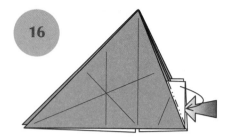

**16**

Reverse-fold,
repeat behind.

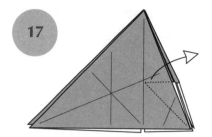

**17**

Pull out the hidden
corner. Repeat behind.

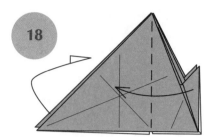

**18**

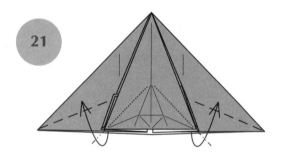

**19**

Make two reverse folds.

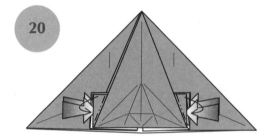

**20**

Make four reverse folds.

**21**

Lift up and refold
along the creases.

**22**

Lift up and refold
along the creases.

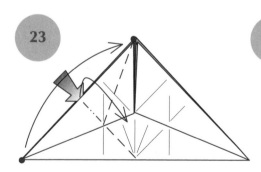

**23**

Lift up so the dots meet
while folding the white
paper to the center.

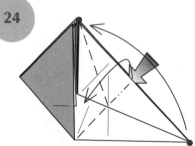

**24**

Repeat step 23
on the right.

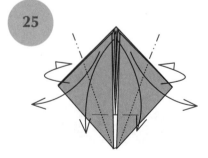

**25**

Kite-fold along the creases from
behind while unfolding and
bringing the hidden flaps down.

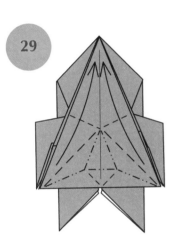
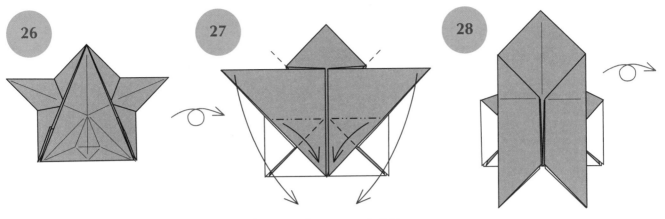

This is similar to squash folds.
Valley-fold along the creases.

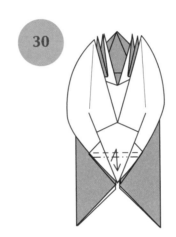
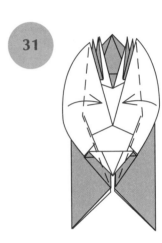

Lift up but do not
flatten at the bottom.

Pleat-fold.

Flatten.

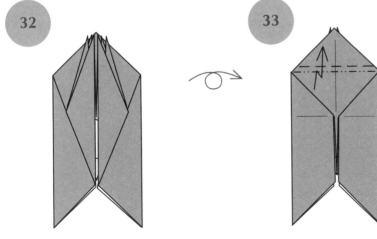
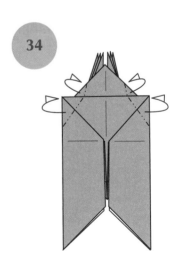

Pleat-fold.

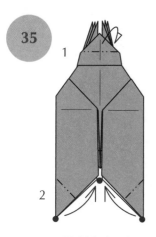

**35**

1. Fold behind.
2. Reverse folds.

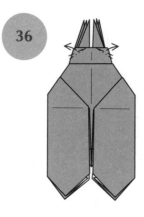

**36**

Form the eyes with
small pleat folds.

**37**

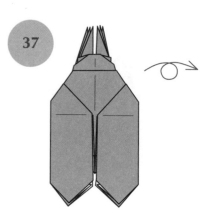

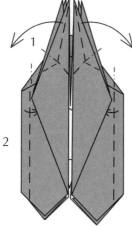

**38**

1. Rabbit-ear all the layers together.
2. Thin the wings.

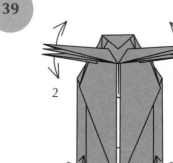
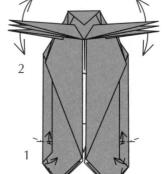

**39**

1. Make thin squash folds.
2. Spread the legs.

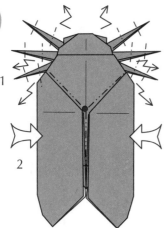

**40**

1. Shape the legs.
2. Lift up at the dot to
   make the cicada 3D.

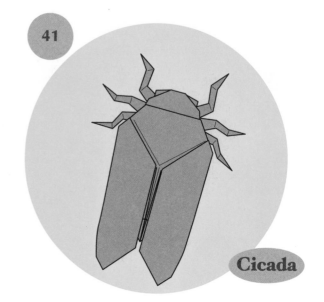

**41**

**Cicada**

# Tarantula

Often portrayed in popular culture as scary, and sometimes as oversized monsters, the reality is that Tarantulas make fun pets. They are gentle, quiet, and do not need much space. With over 900 species, some make for ideal pets. Spiderlings are more active than adults and are fun to watch.

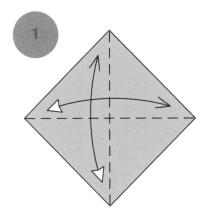

Fold and unfold.

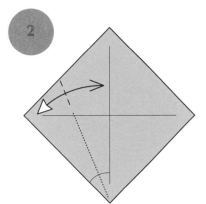

Fold and unfold
on the edge.

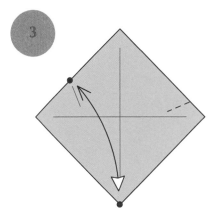

Fold and unfold on the
edge. Rotate 180°.

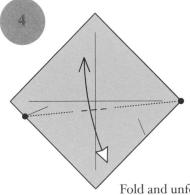

Fold and unfold
along the diagonal.

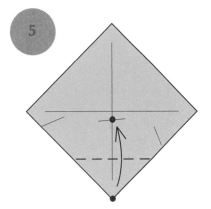

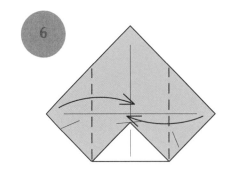

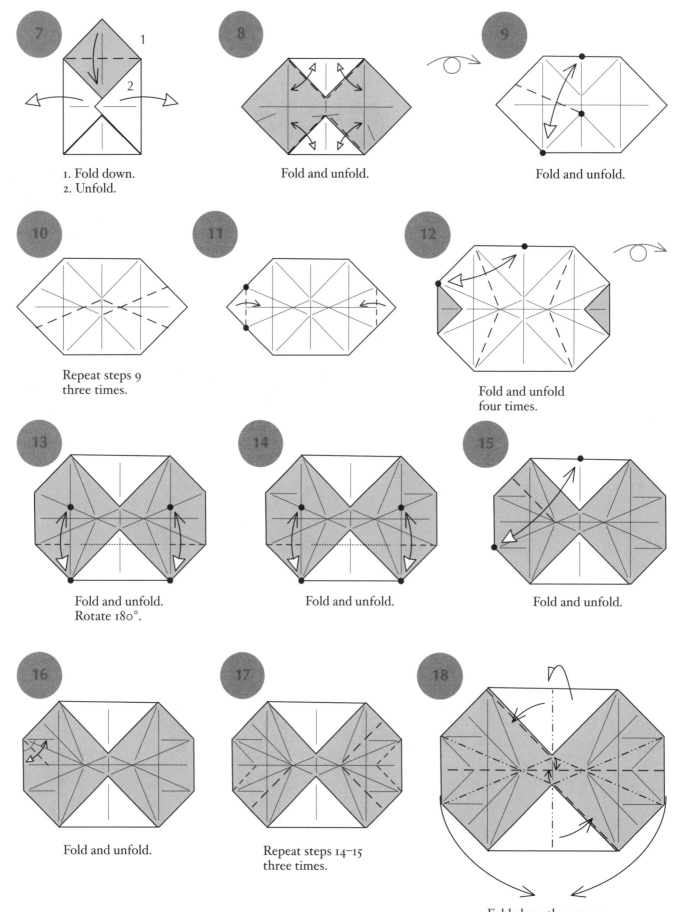

**7**

1. Fold down.
2. Unfold.

**8**

Fold and unfold.

**9**

Fold and unfold.

**10**

Repeat steps 9
three times.

**11**

**12**

Fold and unfold
four times.

**13**

Fold and unfold.
Rotate 180°.

**14**

Fold and unfold.

**15**

Fold and unfold.

**16**

Fold and unfold.

**17**

Repeat steps 14–15
three times.

**18**

Fold along the creases.

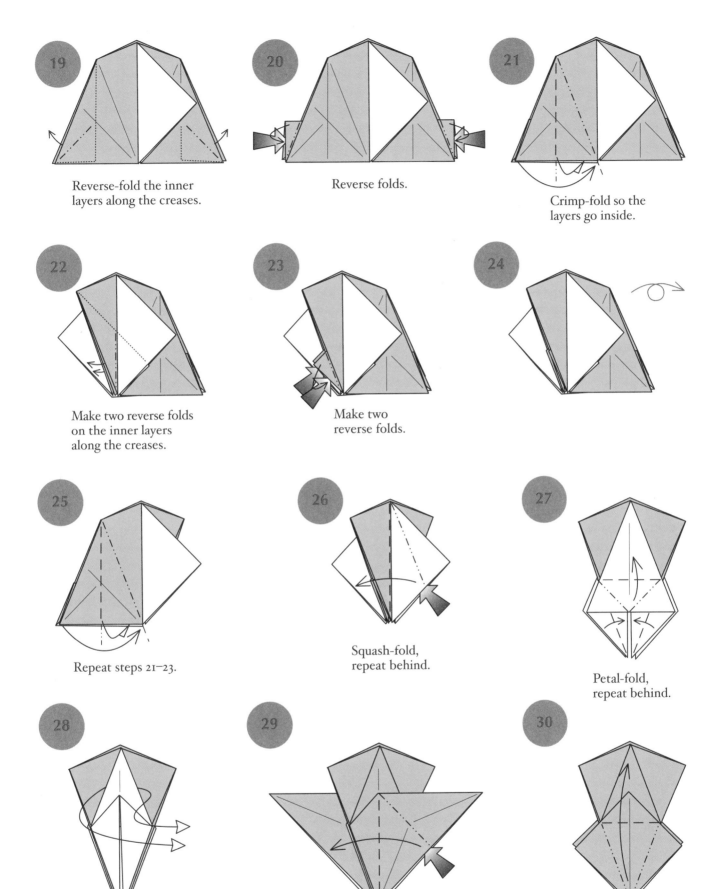

**19** Reverse-fold the inner layers along the creases.

**20** Reverse folds.

**21** Crimp-fold so the layers go inside.

**22** Make two reverse folds on the inner layers along the creases.

**23** Make two reverse folds.

**24**

**25** Repeat steps 21–23.

**26** Squash-fold, repeat behind.

**27** Petal-fold, repeat behind.

**28** Double-unwrap-fold. Repeat behind.

**29** Squash-fold, repeat behind.

**30** Petal-fold, repeat behind.

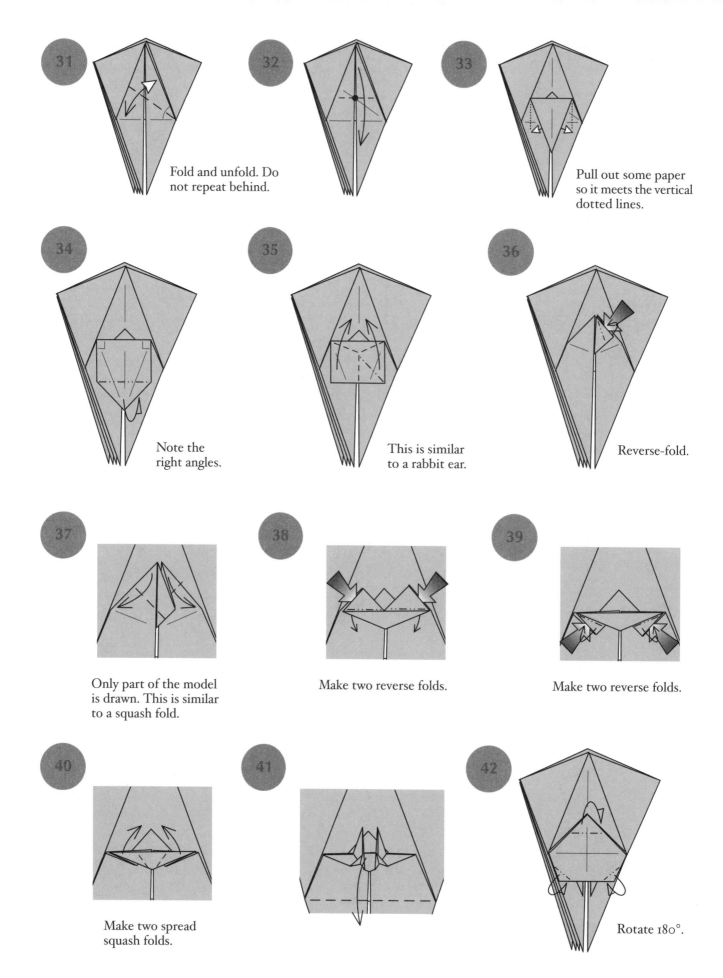

**31** Fold and unfold. Do not repeat behind.

**32**

**33** Pull out some paper so it meets the vertical dotted lines.

**34** Note the right angles.

**35** This is similar to a rabbit ear.

**36** Reverse-fold.

**37** Only part of the model is drawn. This is similar to a squash fold.

**38** Make two reverse folds.

**39** Make two reverse folds.

**40** Make two spread squash folds.

**41**

**42** Rotate 180°.

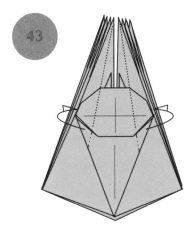

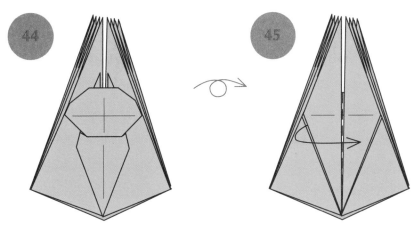

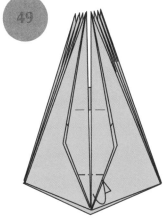

Mountain-fold the second
layer on the left and right.

Fold the top layer.

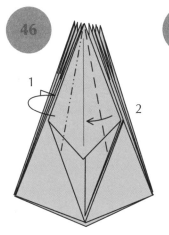

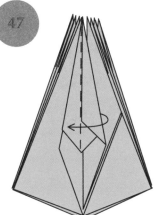

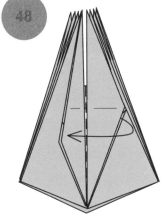

1. Mountain-fold.
2. Valley-fold the top layer.

Repeat steps 45–47
on the right.

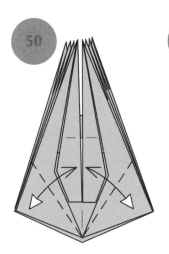

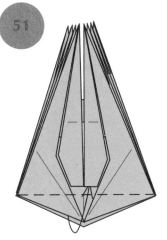

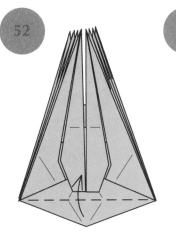

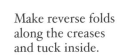

Fold to the center
and unfold.

Tuck one layer
under the flap.

Make reverse folds
along the creases
and tuck inside.

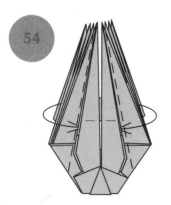

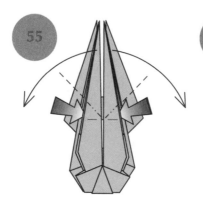

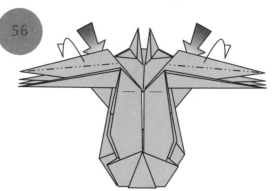

Fold many layers. It is really too thick but it will work out in a few steps.

Reverse-fold all the layers. It is still too thick.

Thin the legs. Make small reverse folds near the head, where the legs start.

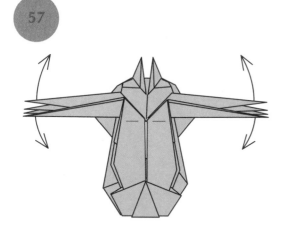

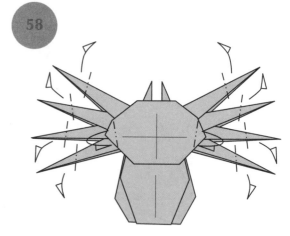

Spread the legs and readjust the folds.

Shape the body and legs.

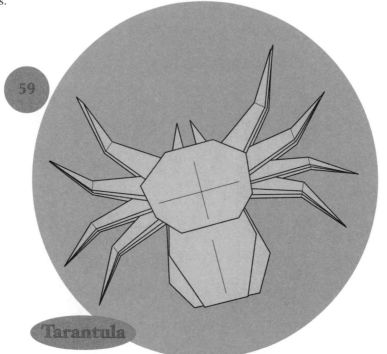

Tarantula